A BIT ON THE SIDE

This book is dedicated to the memory of Graham Rose, who loved his sport and ultimately gave too much. You will not be forgotten.

A BIT ON THE SIDE

*The stirring story of Britain's multiple
World Champion sidecar ace
Steve Webster MBE*

JAN HAVARD

MRP

MOTOR RACING PUBLICATIONS LTD
Unit 6, The Pilton Estate, 46 Pitlake, Croydon CR0 3RY, England

First published 1992

British Library Cataloguing in Publication Data
Havard, Jan
Bit on the Side: Story of Britain's Sidecar World Champion
I. Title
796.7092

ISBN 0-947981-66-7

Typeset in Great Britain by
Ryburn Publishing Services, Halifax, West Yorkshire

Printed in Great Britain by
Hartnolls Limited, Bodmin, Cornwall

CONTENTS

ACKNOWLEDGEMENTS

This book would not have been possible without the kind co-operation of Steve Webster, who inspired me by his on-track performances and gave generously of his time during the research and compilation of the manuscript. My thanks are also due to all the members of Steve's family, who each made significant contributions during my research. Steve's sponsors deserve acknowledgement for the assistance which they gave me in my research, especially Avon and Silkolene. The photographs which accompany the text were supplied by David Goldman, John Colley, Henk Keulemans, Peter Wileman and Kenneth Bray, who deserve the highest praise for the quality of their work.

I would also like to thank David Fern of Donington Park circuit, who went out of his way to assist in the production of this book. In compiling 'A Bit on the Side' I drew many facts and race results from *Motocourse*, edited by Peter Clifford and Michael Scott, and editions of *Rothmans Grand Prix Year Book,* edited by Nick Harris; they were invaluable. Thanks also to Mat Oxley for articles providing excellent background information. To Julian Ryder, Keith Huewen and all the staff at *Eurosport*, a special 'thank you' for their wonderful coverage of the Grands Prix, enabling me to keep up to date with the action at the races I was unable to attend.

I would like to offer particular thanks to my publisher John Blunsden for his unswerving faith and encouragement and for his courage in accepting an unknown quantity in the first place!

Finally to my husband, Nick, for the technical advice, continuous support and encouragement and relentless pounding up and down the A1!

Jan Havard, Sheffield, September 1992

FOREWORD

by Steve Webster MBE

Compiling this book has given me a rare opportunity to look back over my life and to evaluate the things that have happened. In particular it has made me very aware of my 'Championship dash' and of all the people who were caught up in this. I wanted to reach the top as quickly as I could, and indeed being four times World Champion I have now achieved that goal. However, given the chance to start again there are many things that I would approach differently. I realize that in my eagerness to succeed, I have upset a lot of people and on occasion unwittingly caused unhappiness.

I would like to use this Foreword to apologize to the victims of my enthusiasm. I really didn't intend to treat people badly, but I was immature and impulsive when I first started racing. Certainly if I could turn the clock back, I would pace myself a little better. If a young Steve Webster came into my workshop today and asked me how to start in sidecar racing, I know I could give him some very sound advice and save him many problems. If only you could turn the clock back!

People who have helped me to get to the top are too numerous to mention, but I'm sure they know who they are, so they can sit back and enjoy this book and give themselves a well deserved pat on the back. To all those who have helped me to attain the title of 'Four times World Champion', a sincere and heartfelt 'Thank you'. When I lost the World crown, some supporters offered even more staunch help to enable me to recapture the title. Their faith in me and their dependability cannot be valued too highly.

'Thank you' must also be said to my father and Mary for always being there and for providing the voice of reason that I so often used to need, and to Karen, my wife, for supporting me and always having faith in my abilities. I hope that when my children are old enough, they will read and enjoy this book and that it will explain to them why daddy kept disappearing!

I hope that someone will take the time to read this book to Derek Bayley; I know he will smile at the anecdotes recalled. I have dedicated this book to the memory of Graham Rose who tragically lost his life while it was being written. I have continued racing after Graham's death because I know it is what Graham would have wanted. I hope that his family and friends, in sharing this story, will understand a little better why he loved the sport so much.

1

The Haves and Have Nots

'Well done Webbo!' shout the excited fans, their noses pressed up against the paddock fencing, trying to catch a glimpse of the elitist world where only the talented and advantaged are allowed to walk. It is Sunday, September 8, 1991, and a band of dedicated fans have travelled to this, the Circuit du Sarthe, at Le Mans in France, to see their heroes Steve Webster and Gavin Simmons clinch the sidecar World Championship title.

There are some misguided souls who are trying to catch a glimpse of the famous Copacabana and Ipanema beaches, for this is supposed to be the Brazilian Grand Prix – but it isn't! As the Yorkshire stars cruise to an easy third place at Le Mans to clinch the World Championship, the sport is in a state of confusion. The fans who are waving their Union flags and home-made banners are positively delighted that the Brazilian Grand Prix is now being held in France because it meant only a short ferry journey and bike ride to the circuit; a trip to Interlagos would have been out of the question for many supporters, so this change of venue has been a real treat for them.

Why, you may ask, was the Brazilian Grand Prix being held in France? Sadly not for the convenience of the fans, but essentially for political reasons. The whole sport of motorcycle racing was being torn apart by an increasingly bitter struggle for control. Leading 500cc rider Kevin Schwantz, acting as rider's representative, inspected the circuit at Interlagos and found that the promised safety work had not been carried out, so Schwantz and the other riders declared they would not take part. As a result a compromise was found; enter the 'Not the Brazilian Grand Prix'.

Despite the uncertainty surrounding the title of this Grand Prix it produced some memorable racing. Here at Le Mans the 500, 250 and sidecar crowns were claimed by Wayne Rainey, Luca Cadalora and Steve Webster, respectively. Three champions in their own right, but it is there that the similarity ends.

If the great, unloved, but indispensable spectators were allowed into the Grand Prix paddock, they would realize that the fabric of the GP world consists of two classes of citizens, and Webster definitely comes from the wrong side of town. In the GP world there are the haves and the have nots, those whose road to the podium is well supported by finance and works assistance and those, like Steve Webster, who have reached their goals the hard way. Here we have rich and poor mixed together in a heady sporting cocktail. In Rio, slums and cardboard cities stand side by side with grandiose hotels, just as in the GP paddock old transit vans and moth eaten canvas tents look up in envy to luxurious motorhomes. Here, amongst the tangible expressions of sporting superiority, the Webster entourage nestles in what, despite their fourth World Championship, is the less salubrious part of town.

There is a strict pecking order in GP paddocks. The works stars such as Rainey and Cadalora stick together in the stockbroker belt; these are the men who make fortunes out of their pursuit of their chosen sport. They always have the most pleasant end of the paddock in which to parade their sparkling vehicles and the most convenient portion of the pit lane in which to work. As Steve explains, 'You know you are on the right side of the organizers if you are a sidecar team and you get a pit garage. You'd never get Schwantz and Rainey in the same pit because the racing secrets of their teams are so closely guarded. The sidecar lads just aren't like that. I'm happy to share with Rolf [Biland] or Alain [Michel], or any of the other competitors. Some people think we shouldn't be friendly, and on the track we aren't, but in the pits you have to help each other. There are those who think that rivalry hypes up the racing, but I can't pretend, I just don't hate the opposition; that's the way I am and I couldn't alter.'

This relaxed attitude is not evident at the other end of the paddock, where the stresses on the teams are oppressive. Pressure on the riders at this level is overwhelming, the rewards being so magnificent. The Marlboro Roberts Yamaha team with its 40ft articulated transporter containing the six race-prepared YZR500 Yamahas for Wayne Rainey and John Kocinski makes an interesting comparison with the privateers at the other, less fashion-conscious, end of the paddock where Steve Webster is to be found. Whereas the sidecar teams are supportive of each other's needs, the mechanics with the 'big boys' are frantically galloping around the paddock trying to find their own exclusive supply of electricity. 'It really tickles me', says Steve, 'seeing these poor lads fleeing around with a plug in their hands looking for somewhere to stick it!' These same people, at the end of their working day, are still under pressure; they cannot compare experiences with mechanics in another team or have a relaxing pint with them. Even their off-duty time has to be spent with the team so that no confidences are leaked once alcohol has loosened the tongue!

The major players in the 500 and to a lesser extent the 250 classes have moved Grand Prix racing out of the traditional strata of roaming gypsies to a new high tech world of computers, PR grooming and glitzy show business. In the 'upmarket' part of the paddock, great emphasis is placed on designer sunglasses, the latest team fashions and the exact body language expressed in the way you hold your pitboard over the barriers! Marlboro Team Roberts Yamaha, Rothmans Honda and Lucky Strike Suzuki take an army of technical personnel to each Grand Prix. In addition to the vast transporters each team also has its own corporate hospitality entertainment suite, press and publicity facility and on site engineering department. Each rider has at least two bikes at his disposal, tended by anything up to 20 technicians (I have refrained from calling these people mechanics because Grand Prix machines today are no longer looked after by artisans). The modern machine is so complex that it requires the skill of a computer wizard to programme the microprocessors which now govern most aspects of its performance. The latest high-tech fashion is the use of on-board data acquisition equipment, which allows the backroom staff to analyze and adjust everything on the machine from carburation to suspension settings. By changing the microprocessor chip the technical staff can change the entire characteristic of the machine within a few seconds, so ensuring that valuable track time is not wasted.

In contrast, the Webster equipe appears to be living in the Dark

Ages. Although Steve is amongst the most professional of the sidecar racers, he and his small team of Gavin, father Mick and Mary Smith have to carry out every task themselves; it is truly a different world from the 500cc teams. Steve would be the first person to acknowledge the efforts that his tyre and fuel suppliers, Avon and Silkolene, have made in the effort to recapture the world title, but in comparison with the millions of dollars spent by the leading solo runners the budget for a sidecar racer is small change. It has been suggested that Webster's total budget for the 1991 season would not have been sufficient to pay the catering bills of the big three 500 class teams at one Grand Prix!

The competitive instinct spills over from the track to the paddock. One way of scoring points is to have your motorhome driven to the circuit by a gofer while you drive your Porsche or fly in by private executive jet. The top riders have their own motorhome drivers and an army of employees to cater for the team's every need, doing the laundry, chilling the Bollinger, cleaning visors, even overhauling tired and weary bodily parts! But one particular World Champion is not privy to any of these advantages. The truck is driven from circuit to circuit by the family, just as they are responsible for the tools, the repairs and even such basics as the food. The large GP teams have catering services and facilities which are so well organized that a rider need not move out of the GP paddock during the entire four days of the meeting. However, Kevin Schwantz carries a Suzuki jeep in a box trailer, which matches his motorhome, for Mum and girlfriend Amy to go shopping in. Mrs Webster enjoys no such luxury, neither does Steve enjoy the opulent style of trackside living that Schwantz and Rainey are used to. Rainey and Schwantz currently have the showhouses of the paddock; inbuilt washing machines, white leather upholstery, electric curtains and relaxing fibre optic 'stars' on their bedroom ceilings. 'If you are a privateer sidecar team, you also have stars on your bedroom ceiling, real ones that you can see through the hole in your tent!' quips Steve.

Inside the Webster truck everything can be found that is necessary to go racing, without any of the frills. Steve's vehicle is multi-functional; it has to double as living accommodation, workshop, changing room and transporter. The living area has beds, seats and a table, cooker, fridge and shower. Of considerably more importance to Steve is the stock of spare parts and tools that are carried in the workshop section of the converted truck. The living area is also used for the occasional interview demanded by the press. When asked by a well-known journalist why the air conditioning wasn't working, Webster had to admit that his mobile home had not been equipped with such a 'necessity'. However, always eager to be helpful and accommodating, Steve did offer to open another window! His reasoning for not adding such luxuries for the forthcoming season is that it isn't likely to be any hotter in Spain next year than it was this. 'It makes you sweat a bit,' comments Steve cheerfully, 'but I don't spend that much time in the truck anyway. The only time I use the truck is to see journalists or to sleep. In most countries you can eat outside.' Steve feels the money for such a luxury is better employed in providing the team with spare parts for the fragile Krauser engine in the sidecar! Unlike Rainey, Schwantz, Kocinski et al, the Webster entourage actually live in their transporter at the circuits rather than just use it as a convenient resting place between periods of activity at the circuit and the luxury hotels that await at the end of each day's work.

However, living in the suburbs does have its advantages because at least it frees Webster from some of the pressures of GP one-upmanship that other riders have to tolerate. The more advantaged riders are eager to point out that they are doing better than the next person, and in true schoolboy manner rivalry can develop over the exact dimensions of one's acquisitions and can lead to arguments. The 'mine's bigger than yours' debate relates usually to motorhomes and budgets. John Kocinski caused a sensation when he turned up for his first full Grand Prix season with the longest motorhome in the paddock, but his elation soon turned to despair when he was told by Sito Pons that the motorhome was OK, but the doorbell didn't work!

Not only is Kocinski's motorhome the longest in the paddock, it is also probably the cleanest. 'Little John' has a reputation for an obsessive attitude towards cleanliness. Steve describes an incident that occurred earlier in the season, before Kocinski's obsession became so well-known, which illustrates this preoccupation perfectly. Steve was discussing tyre compounds with the Avon technicians when John returned to his motorhome after a practice session; instead of entering his luxury abode. John proceeded to divest himself of leathers, boots, gloves and helmet in a small shelter outside his front door. According to Steve, he left all his clothes in this incongruous structure, which looked like a windbreak, before entering his motorhome in his underpants!

For Steve Webster and especially Gavin Simmons, the events of those last few hours at Le Mans will live in their memories for ever. Despite their relatively underfinanced situation they had achieved a remarkable feat. Alongside the Blue Riband megastars their operation has looked positively meagre, but they have provided close and exciting racing throughout the season and have emerged from the toughest contest in the world with the highest honour that the sport can provide. Their achievement is at least the equal of that of Wayne Rainey, indeed it could be argued that they have achieved considerably more bearing in mind the relative resources available. For Webster this momentous victory ensured that he would take his place in the record books because only Eric Oliver in the Fifties and Rolf Biland in more recent times had earned the same distinction of being sidecar World Champion four times.

It is a shame that the national media has virtually ignored Steve's achievement, whereas when Nigel Mansell was successful in winning the Formula 1 World Championship the hysteria from press and public alike knew no bounds. Steve Webster has recently been Britain's only road-racing World Champion, and there is no other candidate in sight at the moment. So it is fitting that this book is dedicated to the man who, with so little in the way of finance, factory support or influence, has achieved a unique place in motorcycle sport, purely by effort and ability.

What was worrying during the weeks after securing his fourth title was the threat that race fans worldwide might well be denied the opportunity to see the sidecar racers at all during 1992. Throughout the 1990 season there had been a growing rift between the leading 500cc teams and the governing body of the sport (the FIM). This disagreement came to a head midway through the 1991 season when the FIM announced sweeping changes to the regulations governing the 500cc class. Although the controversy centred on the new engine regulations proposed by the FIM, the real reason for the problems facing the sport went much deeper.

It had its roots in the struggle for power and control being waged between the FIM and the International Race Teams Association (IRTA). Basically, the teams wanted to run Grand Prix racing, so ensuring that they had the financial control of the sport, and they cited the FIM as being out of touch with modern racing, and so no longer fit to govern it. As the season drew to a close the prospect of a breakaway World Series loomed ever nearer, and the proposals for this series encompassed all the solo classes, but offered no place for its most dramatic class, the sidecars. Although this branch of the sport is contested by privateers, the standard of racing and the thrilling spectacle of wheel-to-wheel combat surpasses most of the solo class efforts at the majority of Grand Prix meetings. Unfortunately, the sidecar competitors have never been very popular with IRTA due to their appearance and lack of image, and IRTA have stated privately on many occasions that they would like to get rid of any competitor who fails to reach their standard of presentation. This has placed sidecar competitors in a Catch 22 situation, with IRTA making sure that they receive only a fraction of the sum paid to the 500cc competitors, thereby making it even more difficult for them to find the money or influence to improve their image and appearance.

Back in the Le Mans paddock the champagne corks pop in the Rainey camp and the fax machines spew out contracts and sponsorship offers. Rainey is wished a cheery farewell as he boards the Lear Jet and an army of mechanics are briefed for testing at Shah Alam.

Meanwhile, minus a satellite dish on his caravan and devoid of any other ostentatious trappings of success, Webster gazes distractedly at the Euroseries competitors pounding round the circuit. His mind is not on the racing; he is quietly reflecting on the words of one of his major sponsors, the German industrialist Roland Munch: 'Forward, forward, the Championship is won but you must plan for next year'. So rather than joining in the celebrations with Gavin and Julie Simmons and their children, and visitors such as the ever friendly Niall Mackenzie, Steve stands to one side pondering the future. All he feels is a great sense of relief. The spectre of the World Series hangs like the Sword of Damocles over him; he knows he should be as happy as the rest of the team, but the prospect of not being able to race next year is too big a burden. As he turns the key in the ignition of the truck and heads for the ferry, he knows that the same nagging question will keep tormenting him all the way back to Easingwold, the question that Roland Munch put to him: 'What next?'

2
A Star is Born

Before we look forward, let us look back. Back to a snowy morning in January 1960, when this four-times World Champion first appeared on the scene.

The Webster family have their roots in York, and at the time of Steve's birth, Mick and Sylvia were living at New Earswick, two miles north of York city centre. New Earswick is a village which was built by Joseph Rowntree, of confectionery fame, to house his workers. Most of its inhabitants are employed by the Rowntrees factory and therefore know each other extremely well. This creates a secure community atmosphere in the village, one in which Steve felt lucky to spend his childhood. New Earswick is the kind of place which is a haven for children, who can roam far and wide free from danger, safe in the knowledge that they know so many people to whom they can turn if any problem arises.

Unusually, Mick was not employed by the Rowntree factory, and at the time of Steve's birth he worked as an aircraft engineer at Hawker Siddeley. Sylvia, however, did and still does work in the offices at Rowntrees. They already had one son, Kevin, who was 22 months old when Steve was born. Their closeness in age led to an inevitable closeness in many other areas and they grew up together sharing toys, hobbies and friends and, later, their love of racing.

In a sense, racing even played its part in the earliest moments of Steve Webster's life as his father Mick had been attending a racing club presentation and dinner on the night that he arrived. When Sylvia realized that an addition to the family was imminent, several frantic phone calls were made and the expectant father was located and rushed home in time for the birth in the early hours of Monday morning, January 7, 1960.

Steve, it would seem, was a healthy and placid baby, and his parents report that there was nothing in his early childhood to indicate the path that he eventually would take. It does seem, though, that the future World Champion had an early desire to 'set the world on fire'!

Sylvia Webster recollects, 'Anything to do with fire seemed to fascinate him. Even as a very small toddler all his socks would be singed at the toes. As soon as you let him out of your sight, he would go and push his toes through the fireguard until his socks began to burn. He didn't have any socks that weren't scorched. He was always an inquisitive and mischievous child, constantly meddling in things. He had a daring little friend called Nigel, and together I nicknamed them 'the firebugs'. One day, Steve was playing with Nigel – they were two of a kind, always grubby and up to mischief – and Steve came in and asked for a bucket of water. Assuming this was part of some game I obliged, but was surprised when he quickly reappeared and asked for another bucketful, then another and another. By bucket number five I began to get suspicious and inquired "what are you playing at, dear?". "Oh, just putting a hedge fire out, Mum", replied Steve. Sylvia says it was quite some time before her neighbours spoke to her.

Nigel, also known as Joddy, was also eager to demonstrate to Steve the properties that petrol has for causing a blaze. He had seen some careless adult encouraging a bonfire by pouring petrol on it. Steve watched with interest as Nigel lit a fire using petrol from the lawn mower, but he was not so impressed when Nigel, trying to stamp out his successful blaze, set his shoes on fire!

Electricity also captured the young Webster's attention. He tried at the age of two to fuse himself to the National Grid by inserting a nail file in between a plug socket and the wall; luckily he made a contact between the live and earth pins, fusing the whole house but at least remaining alive. He also developed a communication system with the house opposite, which consisted of wires and tins and a Websterized morse code.

But Steve's daring approach to the elements was not mirrored when it came to tackling the unexpected. Like many children in the Sixties, he encountered that weekly test of one's nerves: dare he, or dare he not watch Dr Who? 'I'm sure he really wanted to watch it, but as soon as the theme music came on he would dive behind the settee and watch from there,' laughs Sylvia.

Although nowdays few could dispute Steve's love of speed, one of his early encounters with life in the fast lane left him feeling less than glowing. When he was in nursery school, he was chosen because of his good looks and blond hair to be a page boy to the Carnival Queen in the New Earswick village carnival. Smartly turned out in a blue satin suit, young Webster boarded the back of the local coal merchant's lorry, duly trimmed up for the occasion. Proud parents waved him off on his 5mph tour of the village and the happy toddler cheerfully waved back. But it was not such a happy face that greeted his family as he returned from this early public tour of duty. The young Webster was extremely green, suffering badly from travel sickness, an affliction that has remained with him to this day; he is still unable to map read in a moving vehicle or to travel for long distances in the rear seat of a car. 'If we are off for a night out and there are girls in the car with strong perfume on, I have to travel with the window open, which isn't always popular in the cold weather. Despite the thousands of miles I covered, racing and travelling, I'm still not a very good traveller,' Steve admits.

Steve always loved to help his parents; he would help his Mum to decorate and both he and Kevin loved to help Mick in the garage where he spent hours renovating bikes and cars. Mick was an indulgent father, the kind who just left the boys to play as they wished, and one day, at the tender age of two, Steve had his moment of glory in Dad's garage. He had watched Mick put the finishing touches to a renovation paint job on a Morris Minor. Mick is a perfectionist and Sylvia recalls, 'The car looked a picture, its bodywork was smooth and glistening.' Steve loved to watch his father, and the infant Webster watched intently as dad carefully applied the paint. Eager to help, Steve picked up a brush and began to 'paint' the other side of the vehicle. Eventually, father and apprentice son met, Mick having painted his side, Steve having doused his carefully with thinners. Mick's reaction was inevitable: 'I've just bloody painted that! Sylvia, come and get your son out of here!'

Steve loved to play with Kevin's toys, their difference in age small enough to make them behave more like twins than brothers. Steve's favourite toys were anything that belonged to Kevin. This partly came from an admiration of big brother and partly from the fact that Kevin cared for and polished his toy cars, put them away in neat, ordered rows, whereas Steve was an untidy child, a trait inherited from his father. Steve's cars were mangled and well-used. Each boy had a drawer for their possessions; Kevin's drawer was clean and tidy, his toys carefully placed inside, but Steve's was a jumble, with everything just thrown in. The boys loved to race their Dinky Toy cars around the carpet, Kevin's treasures beautifully race prepared, Steve's all scratched and battered.

But although Steve's handling of his toys left much to be desired, his treatment of people has always been caring and sensitive. A childhood friend, Beverley recounts, 'Steve was always popular with everyone. I came to the village when I was about eight and I made friends through Steve. He was always kind and considerate.'

Steve's kindness was not limited to people, for both he and Kevin loved animals. One winter they acquired a kestrel. Another boy in the village had begun to raise the chick but then found he couldn't manage anymore and wanted to find a good home for the bird. Steve brought it home to live in the kitchen. Sylvia was very tolerant of the visitor eating the kitchen mat and sleeping in a box on the floor. The boys nursed the bird back to health and took it for flying practice on the school playing field. They were delighted when a year after it had been set free, the bird came back to visit them.

Steve enjoys horse riding and was often taken by his aunt and uncle to ride. Little did he know but this was a useful babysitting routine in order to let Mick and Sylvia pursue their hobby of grasstrack racing. Mick would ride to the track on his Villiers machine and Sylvia would ride pillion. Sylvia would have a rucksack full of sprockets on her back, ready to convert the bike to race specification once they arrived at the circuit.

School was a necessary interruption of easygoing days riding his pushbike and developing his other childhood passion that was nearly as all-consuming as his fascination for fire, his propensity for tunnelling! Webster, Stephen, as school registers say, did not especially like school but he went willingly because he realized it was something he had to do.

He found learning easy, had a flair for maths, but was held back by the introduction of the ITA approach to reading, a system of using linguistic symbols for words, which proved to be a disastrous failure and was soon scrapped by the Education Authority. This educational experiment did no favours for Steve and his counterparts, and in Steve's case it has affected his spelling and led him to avoid putting pen to paper.

The sound of the school bell was a welcome one to young Webster's ears. He would tear away from the New Earswick Primary School, race home to grab his bike and pound up and down the local tip. The tip had become grassed over and was made into a race track by the local lads.

Indeed, the Webster childhood was a happy, contented one, and Steve was never more contented than when he was tunnelling. To this day there are relics of Steve's past in his mother's garden; a heavy porcelain sink buried several feet down is a remnant of a Webster den. His dens and tunnels were many and varied in their construction. Beverley recalls 'Steve spent ages taking the insides out of an old television set. The idea was that you would crawl through the set into another world and that this world would be reached down a tunnel.' Perhaps all that exposure to Dr Who did have some effect after all!

Even at secondary school, break times were spent, not smoking behind the bike sheds, but down manholes under classroom floors exploring tunnels. There are even tunnels at the factory of Joseph Rowntree that have been visited by our mole. 'Luckily' smiles Steve, 'I've always been good at getting away with things. Once I was down a tunnel at school and my friend was 'doggying' out for me, he hadn't been able to warn me that the Deputy Headmistress was waiting for me when I surfaced from my tunnel. This boy was one of life's natural scapegoats because if anyone got into trouble, it was him. Despite his protests that the whole operation wasn't his idea, the teacher refused to believe him and he got the punishment. I managed to look innocent and fortunately escaped punishment, despite being the instigator of the expedition.'

On one occasion Rowntrees suffered structural damage when Webster refused to believe he was at the end of his tunnel and he attacked the wall with a hammer. 'We would spend break times exploring passageways that had been blocked off some time ago. One day we didn't believe we had reached the end of one particular tunnel and demolished a wall with hammers and chisels!' reports our tunneller.

Although the passion for burrowing is totally of Steve's own volition, he admits that he is easily led. 'I've often gone along with things that really I've thought risky or plain silly, but I find myself agreeing and often ending up in hot water. Once I was encouraged to ride my bike round a neighbour's field and found myself staring down the barrel of a gun. I was riding where I shouldn't have been and this other lad was shooting an air rifle at something in a tree. Unfortunately he shot me and I ended up in hospital having a pellet taken out of my chin.' Steve didn't seem to learn from the experience, for many years later, a dare in a bar at Hockenheim similarly led to several days in hospital. 'It was when I first started racing and it was all a bit of a laugh being out with the lads, etc. There's a trick you can do lying on chairs, your head on one chair and your feet on another. The chairs get further and further apart and are passed over and under you. I fell off and hurt my neck so badly that I ended up in hospital. I really thought I'd broken my neck. It still gives me trouble!' Mick takes up the story here and remarks that it isn't only his friends who lead Steve on. 'The upshot of this game in the bar was that Steve was admitted to hospital, convinced he had broken his neck. The hospital, deutschemarks registering in their eyes, were happy to corroborate this notion, telling him he must stay in the hospital for several weeks and pay for his treatment. Steve is very cautious about his health and immediately agreed. We knew that he wasn't as seriously injured as he had feared, so we rescued him from financial ruin and got him back to the race track. I'm afraid Steve would have believed them if they'd told him he needed permanent hospitalization!'

Although the juvenile Webster had shown no early signs of becoming one of this country's most accomplished motorsports stars, he was involved in the dramatic and colourful world of motorcycle racing from an early age. From babyhood, the infant Webster would be taken along to grasstrack meetings to see his father race.

Mick Webster was a very successful grasstrack racer, winning the British Sidecar Grasstrack Championship on three occasions, and competing in many branches of the sport. Indeed his experience encompassed such diverse aspects of the sport as trials, motocross – known as scrambling in those days – and road racing, in addition to his grasstracking exploits. The whole family would accompany Mick on his weekend forays to muddy fields, where he would invariably carry off the major trophies, riding his self-built machines with a style and pace that were to become the hallmarks of his son over a decade later. Mick's experience of racecraft, coupled to his engineering expertise and knowledge of racing, gave an invaluable boost to the second-generation racer when he eventually started to follow his destiny.

Steve's first 'racing' machine was built for him by his doting father when he was just six years old. Mick had had a sizeable accident on one of his grasstrack outfits and had broken his collarbone, so, being bored he set out to construct a junior sidecar outfit by converting an old moped. He managed to build this with just one hand, his other strapped up because of his injury. Having the use of just one arm, however, did not deter Webster senior, as he cut and welded the previously innocent and harmless machine to produce a miniature racer which the two brothers thrashed around a local field.

The competition between Kevin and Steve to see who could lap their makeshift circuit fastest became quite intense, leading to numerous spills and honing of the competitive instinct. It became common practice for the boys to take their outfit to the meetings where Mick was racing, and they would 'demonstrate' their skills on the circuit during the lunch intervals! The piping voices of the Webster boys would be heard above the purr of the engine: 'Let me have a go, hurry up, let's swap over!' Whoever was passengering would be urging the other boy to change places. Both boys wanted to be the rider.

The scaled down sidecar outfit was the first of several motorized devices that Mick created for his sons. Later machines included a solo motorbike that Steve used to ride along the side of a disused railway line. Being a concerned and caring parent, Mick would telephone people along the line to check on Steve's progress, making sure that the infant prodigy was safe and that he wasn't being too much of a nuisance!

Mick Webster was a very accomplished racer. At one grasstrack meeting he won the 250cc solo, 500cc solo and sidecar events on the same day on three different machines! Today, when asked who the best sidecar racers were and who were his early heroes, Steve unhesitatingly says 'my dad!'

These hectic but happy teenage years were marred when Steve succumbed to a serious illness. At the age of 13 he had peritonitis and nearly lost his fight for life. 'He came in one Sunday night', Sylvia remembers, 'and said he didn't feel well. I thought at first it was a tummy bug.Three days later he was very ill. I was debating whether to call the doctor, or whether I was fussing. I went up to look at Steve and there were beads of perspiration all over his face. He shouldn't be like that, I thought, so I rang the doctor. As it was night time, it wasn't our own doctor who came but a locum. He felt Steve's stomach and rang for an ambulance straight away. Steve's appendix had burst and he needed an emergency operation.'

An agonizing few days passed for Mick and Sylvia Webster. Steve survived the operation but complications set in and Steve developed adhesions on his bowel. Several operations followed over a period of three years, and Steve eventually made a full recovery, but he is still prone to gastric problems, especially if he is under stress.

This period of illness disrupted his education, and although he did return to the Joseph Rowntree secondary modern school, he was keen to leave as soon as he was old enough, aware that his absence due to illness had caused him to fall a long way behind his peers. Easter of 1976 couldn't come soon enough.

3

Teenage Tearaway

At last the great day came and Webster was able to escape from the Joseph Rowntree secondary school, leaving by the conventional route, not via one of his many tunnels. He was now faced with one of the first major decisions of his life: 'What next?'

The logical progression for a school leaver in York is to seek a position at the city's largest and most prestigious employer, Joseph Rowntree, and Steve was about to exchange one connection with the late confectioner for another. He obtained an application form for a job at the factory and found he could choose between an apprenticeship for an electrician, a plumber or a fitter. Despite – or perhaps because of – the episode with the nail file and the wiring, the job of electrician had no special appeal for Steve and after discussing the options with his parents, it was thought that Steve's aptitude for fiddling with things mechanical would be best channelled into becoming a fitter.

The first weeks at work rather resembled starting at a new school. 'I felt rather uneasy when I started at work,' Steve remembers. 'At least at school I knew everybody and you knew the routine, but here I was catapulted into a whole new world. My first year at work, in fact, was to be spent at technical college, learning the trade of fitter, so it was like school all over again, but a school where I didn't know a soul. At first I felt very shy.'

However, the time passed uneventfully and Steve worked hard, being eager to get to grips with practising his trade. After the initial year at college, Steve went to work in the factory, but he still attended college on day release and for night school, as the total training for a fitter spanned three years. If the college world had reminded Webster of school, his impressions of those first few weeks at the factory must have resembled being in an institution for delinquents! At Rowntrees, as in many firms, the initiation procedures for newcomers are many and varied! His first job was to follow an engineering drawing to produce 'something very special for face testing'. 'I was anxious to create a good impression,' beams Webster. 'The drawing was very detailed, with measurements down to fine divisions and tolerances into thousandths, etc. Some parts were to have machined ends, and all the measurements were critical, as I was constantly reminded. I worked meticulously on this project and having finished it I asked what exactly it was for. I had worked for two days designing an Irish dog carrier!'

This was only one of the many fool's errands on which Webster was sent. 'I think I spent my first six months at Rowntrees pursuing one con after another. I've queued up for tins of assorted holes, searched for double-headed sweeping brushes, and of course I've been for a long stand. I am so gullible! Jeff, the person I was working with, told me very straightfaced to go to Lenny in the stores and ask for a long stand. He stressed "don't come back without it, lad". Being new you just accept that this is a serious part of the job. I also thought he might want to see if I was conversant with the stores procedure. To get an item from the stores you have to hand in a brass disc and this is hung on a hook to indicate what you've borrowed. I was taking it all in, you see, trying to be impressive. "Hello, Lenny", I said, "I've come for a long stand." "Right you are", said Lenny, then he took my disc and disappeared. It went very quiet, and it seemed like most people had disappeared; perhaps it was tea break? I stood there and stood there. I must have been there a good half an hour before I realized something was up. I was a delight to play tricks on, and still am in a way, as I never seem to know when I'm being set up.'

Even if you have a long-standing reputation as a practical joker, you are unlikely to alert Steve, as another incident during these first few weeks indicated. 'The plumbers at Rowntrees were notorious for dousing other workers with buckets of water. I suppose they thought that if they had to work in wet conditions a lot, why should the rest of us get off scot-free. One guy I worked with, a renowned prankster, decided we should get even with the plumbers, or so he told me. The plumbers had their tea-breaks high up in the building and would often shower somebody on the way down the stairs. I was detailed to be look-out, and when the plumbers were about I was to give my mate the nod. I ought to have realized that my little friend was in league with the plumbers, and as I leaned over the staircase to watch for the plumbers, it was me who got the dousing! When I recounted the episode to the other apprentices they said, "Well him, you know he's the worst of the lot!" I'm obviously too trusting by far,' says Webster.

There was one occasion, though, during those early days at Rowntrees, when Steve had the last laugh. Apprentices were only allowed to work overtime on Saturday mornings and Steve was always short of cash, so his ears pricked up when he heard Tony Ford asking if any lads wanted to make an easy £20 for an hour's work. 'I was thinking that it would buy a new tyre for the car' says Steve, 'so I nipped over to Tony and asked him what this job entailed. Tony explained "Well, it's not actually at the factory; Larry, one of the fitters, does this job in his spare time, it's cleaning the pipes of York Minster's organ. Larry can't make it this time, though. It has to be done very early in the morning, as the organ is used through the day. The pipes get very sooty, you see. It'll take two of you, though, one to push the brushes through and one up at the top to pull them out". The more Tony described this job, the more I thought that it was easy money.

"'OK", I volunteered, "I'll do it, but where do I get the keys from?" I was told that I'd have to be there for 4.30am and that the key was at Brockfield.

At 3.30am on the following Sunday I picked up Graham Harrison, a friend, and we drove to Brockfield. It did occur to me as I was motoring along that Brockfield is a bloody long way from York Minster and if the key was needed in an emergency it wasn't very sensible. But still, mine was not to reason why; my role in all this was to make an easy tenner! We pulled up at the given address but I couldn't get right outside, so I parked down the road and told Graham to nip out and get the key. Graham knocked on the door, and after much persistent hammering managed to rouse a bleary-eyed fellow, who shouted expletives at Graham from his bedroom window.

'I could hear Graham explaining, "I've come for the key".

"What bloody key?", came the agitated reply.

"To get into the Minster to clean the organ pipes", pleaded Graham.

"F**k off, you maniac" came the firm reply, and the window slammed shut.

'Graham dashed back to the car. "I know who that was", I told him, "it's one of the managers from work, I've been set up here". Graham didn't say a word, at least nothing that could be put into print; his prospect of an easy £10 down the drain, and here he was wide awake at 4.15am on a Sunday morning!' However, this is not the end of the story. Graham was not a Rowntrees employee, and Webster had not been spotted by the manager. Graham is a very distinctive character and always easy to pick out in a crowd because of his shock of red hair. The next day at work, Tony Ford and his fellow conspirators couldn't wait to hear how Steve had got on cleaning the Minster pipes.

'Have a good morning at the Minster then?', inquired Tony nearly bursting with suppressed amusement.

'Oh, I didn't go,' replied Webster.

Tony's face fell; he was just about to ask why Steve had changed his mind when the manager flew in. 'Where's that red-haired lunatic that came hammering on my door in the middle of the night going on about organ pipes and keys?'

'Red-haired?' queried Tony,

'Yes, I'd know him anywhere', fumed the boss.

Webster smiled sweetly. 'See Tony, I told you I didn't go.'

One distinct advantage of becoming a wage earner was that it provided the necessary capital to be able to learn to drive. Mick had long since left his position as an aircraft engineer and had set up on his own as a motor engineer, his one time hobby having developed into a successful business. Sadly, by this stage of Steve's adolescence, his parents had become divorced, but were both happy in new relationships. Steve would visit his father at Flawith and admire the numerous vehicles left with him for renovation. Mick promised Steve that as soon as he was old enough to drive, he would do up a car specially for him, and once Steve was 16, preparations took shape for the future Webster conveyance.

Minis were very much in vogue in the mid-Seventies and,

inspired by Silver Jubilee year, Steve chose a red, white and blue colour scheme for his first vehicle, little realizing that his patriotism – and skill – would be honoured by a trip to Buckingham Palace a decade later.

It took 12 months to renovate the Mini fully and Steve was delighted when people stopped him and admired the car, mistaking it for a limited edition Jubilee Mini.

Driving lessons went well. Steve had driven cars on private land from the age of 13. 'I could get a car on two wheels and do handbrake turns like there was no tomorrow. Stopping at zebra crossings and observing a 30mph limit proved a little harder,' reflects Steve.

However, Webster failed his first test on undue hesistancy, but passed two months later. Brother Kevin thought all his birthdays had come at once when he sat his test. The boy's uncle is a driving instructor in York, so many of the examiners were well known to the Websters. When Kevin took his test the examiner he had was an old family friend; Kevin had seen him dozens of times at family gatherings. He got in the car and greeted Kevin like a long-lost chum, inquiring 'How's your mum, Kevin? What's your dad up to? Do you still live in New Earswick?', and so on. Kevin thought this driving test lark was going to be a piece of cake. The examiner nattered on all through the test and very soon they pulled up back at the test centre. 'Well Kevin, it's been lovely to see you again, I'm sorry that you've failed your test, take care now.' Kevin was sick as a parrot!

The first year on the road was a very turbulent one for the boy racer. He had only been driving three weeks when he had his first accident, which involved unceremoniously punting his father's XJ6 up the rear end. 'I was following my dad back to his garage and as he turned up the drive he saw a truck reversing down the drive. Dad slammed the Jaguar into reverse, but I didn't react quickly enough and I ran right into the back of him. Or you could say he backed into me! I came off worst, my beloved Mini had its front all squashed in, but the XJ6 was unscathed.'

Steve rounded off an evening celebrating his engagement to first wife Jill by doing an unintentional victory roll in his Cortina 1600E. Fortunately no-one was hurt. On another occasion he skidded on the ice near his mother's home and demolished several road cones and lamps, completely writing off his car, but again he emerged intact.

Friday night was traditional race night for Steve and a group of other Earswick hot shoes, who also owned Minis. The starting grid was the local level-crossing, the red lights provided by the crossing gates. As they opened, the red haze came down and the race was underway. These Grands Prix resulted in many a dented wing and buckled bumper.

Grands Prix were also held at the 'Circuit du Rowntree', in the cellars under the factory, not with road cars but with Yale trucks. Tracks were set out in the cellars and race-prepared trucks brought out from their hiding places. If a truck handled especially well it would be taken from normal duties and secreted away. However, this 'championship' was discovered by the management and after what Webster describes as a rumpus, was withdrawn from the racing calendar.

But these halcyon days of boyish recklessness were soon to come to an end when Webster, at the tender age of 18, decided to marry. Brother Kevin had married in 1978 and Mick had given Kevin £500 as a wedding present to help him to set up home. Always being fair, Mick pointed out that when Steve got married he could also have £500.

Steve had been friendly since schooldays with Jill. She was an exceedingly pretty girl and as children she and Steve had been the best of friends. Encouraged by the incentive of £500, Jill and Steve very quickly found a house and announced to Mick and Sylvia that they, too, were to be wed.

But although the two were the best of friends, they did not have the basis to sustain a long-term relationship. Steve had fallen into the trap of mistaking friendship for love. The relationship did not go well, each began to spend more and more time with their own friends, and Steve started to watch racing frequently at the weekends.

Graham Harrison teamed up with Steve to go to Carnaby and to other tracks such as Mallory Park and Oliver's Mount. 'I had a few heroes to follow in those days,' recalls Steve, 'including my dad, of course, who had been Grasstrack National Champion and had also competed in road racing. I can remember watching him at Mallory Park, and the grandstands were full. To me, he looked really wonderful: he had a Triumph bike, white with a blue stripe on it. I can remember to this day that it was number 26 and all the riders were the same in black leathers. There was another time when I went to watch him at Scarborough and his carburettor fell off! He went straight on along the straight and the spectators had to dive for cover – they were all shaking their fists at him! I had heroes in grasstrack, people who had been nice to me when I was a child, and now I was old enough to admire them for their talent – people like Ginger Lofthouse, Dennis Teasdale and Dave Hunter.

'One day Graham and I went to Oliver's Mount to watch the Cock of the North road races. We were perched in a tree to get a better view and as Barry Sheene came by, he appeared to wave at us. I thought it was marvellous, Barry Sheene had waved at me! It was only when I raced myself that I realized he hadn't been waving at all, merely acknowledging another rider.

'Graham and I spent our evenings sampling York's supply of ale and weekends travelling far and wide watching racing. I began to think about competing myself; I had tasted the thrills of competitive racing once before but the experience had not ended happily. My father lives with a lady called Mary Smith. Mary was eager to become involved in racing and she entered a grasstrack ladies race in a grasstrack car. I was around 13 at the time and went regularly with my father and Mary to grasstrack car races organized by Tony Drummond. I was absolutely dying to have a go at driving but of course I wasn't old enough. One of my dad's friends had a bright idea, that I should be entered in the ladies' race as Stefanie Webster, after all, in a helmet who would know?! So, the plot went ahead and, duly kitted out in leathers and helmet, I shot off in the car. I hadn't got far when I turned the beast over and the marshals came rushing to my assistance. I was determined that under no circumstances were they going to remove my helmet. I hung there, upside-down, protesting that I was fine. "Take your helmet off, love", the marshal urged. "No, no", I squeaked, "I'm fine, just turn the car the right way up please and I'll be on my way". However, the marshal was not prepared to do this. Instead he promptly undid my seat belt, causing me to slip and do more damage than the original accident had done, and then he eased off my helmet: "Ay, you're not a lass!" he remarked. What can you do when someone states the obvious, so I smiled sweetly!'

Steve's first taste of sidecar action came at about the same time as his attempt at transvestism; his father had constructed a grasstrack outfit using a Hillman Imp car engine as motive power. The Imp engine was a development of the Coventry Climax FWE fire pump unit fitted to most of this country's fire engines. It wasn't used to drive the fire engine, but merely to power the lift pump that forced water at high pressure through the firemen's hoses. This type of engine was very popular in many forms of four-wheel motorsport, being a light-alloy overhead-camshaft design with the ability to reach high revolutions and with plenty of tuning potential. The use of such an engine in three-wheelers became commonplace in the late Seventies, but Mick's early pioneering efforts seemed to have a less than beneficial effect on his passengers! The extra horsepower generated by this car engine was causing passengers to loose their grip under the violent acceleration, and Mick was beginning to run out of partners; for some reason, they didn't relish the idea of being deposited on their backsides!

In an effort to make the 'beast' more controllable Mick was conducting some private testing at a nearby airfield. After his regular passenger had been deposited on the floor for the umpteenth time, and was refusing to get on board again, the teenaged offspring volunteered his services! Naturally Mick was not too keen on this idea, but in the interests of science he relented, vowing not to get too enthusiastic with the throttle. Steve's ability to hang on to the bucking and writhing machine impressed all present; even when his father gave the outfit full throttle the youngster remained in the chair and in control of his actions.

Steve's success in staying on board the 'unrideable' machine, when so many others had failed, became a local folklore tale, recounted many times with varying and increasing amounts of exaggeration, over numerous pints, in countless hostelries around the York area. Yet strangely, this outstanding success did not instantly catapult young Steve into a life on the motorcycle racing circuits. He seemed to be unaffected by this experience and indeed did not show any further interest in the sport for some considerable time.

However, his interest in the sport was reawakened on one of his visits to a track with Graham. 'Deep down inside I thought this was something I could do. It was something I would enjoy and I felt, I don't know why, that I could be really good at it. All the way home from the race meeting Graham and I talked about nothing else. We would get a sidecar outfit and we would race. I was filled with excitement. I had overlooked the practicalities of the situation; the fact that neither Graham nor myself had the necessary finance to begin to race. It didn't matter, I was gripped by an ambition, one which would change my life.'

4

Getting Started

Steve couldn't wait to tell his father what he and Graham intended to do. He was full of his plans, but Mick had to bring the fledgling World Champion down to earth, by pointing out the finance needed and Steve's responsibilities to the new Mrs Webster. Meanwhile, Graham Harrison was also having cold water poured on his plans, and it soon became clear to our would-be pairing that the sidecar combination of Webster and Harrison was not to be.

Quite by chance Steve related his plans and ideas to Kevin. Of late, Kevin had been very preoccupied with his young family, but at the mention of racing he became very excited. It turned out that Kevin would be keen to try sidecar racing but finance was still a problem.

'Well,' said Mick, 'perhaps there is something I can do. Ever since you were small, I've treated you the same and for that reason I wouldn't help one of you if I couldn't do the same for the other. If you are going to go into racing, a sidecar is ideal because that way I can help both of you.'

The brothers were overjoyed; this was the start of tremendous support from Mick, both financial and moral. The moral support continues to this day and Steve is proud to say he has been able to redress the financial balance in recent years.

Apart from being in a position to help the boys get started in sidecar racing, Mick also felt that this was a way that he could keep them safe. In the unpredictable world of racing, accidents do happen, and although Mick could not prevent the inevitable, he felt that by his involvement he could cover most eventualities and keep his flesh and blood as safe as humanly possible.

No sooner said than done. Once the family Webster had decided that the racing operation was to go ahead a machine was acquired. After studying the small advertisements in *Motor Cycle News*, a complete outfit was purchased at a reasonable price. Included in the sale were several engines and many spare parts. The budding racers thought that they had the equipment to go racing with but they very soon discovered that the old, outdated Fidderman chassis would require a lot of work to make it raceworthy. Some updating would also be necessary to make it competitive. The brothers continued to attend race meetings during this period of renovation, but the emphasis had changed. Instead of standing at the trackside watching cornering techniques, they could now be found wandering around the paddock, taking a much closer interest in how the successful outfits were put together. Their interest in the actual racing now seemed to be almost non-existent as they examined the machines of their 'rivals to be' in the most intimate detail, often being caught in the act of measuring some design feature, or taking close-up photographs of components that could be adapted to their own outfit.

One of the most startling conclusions that they came to was that their secondhand machine was of the old-fashioned 'conventional' design where the driver sat on the bike. All the modern machines were of the 'kneeler' type where the driver was almost lying down on the outfit. 'As soon as we saw the variation in design, of kneeling on the outfit, we went home and started sawing our outfit apart,' says Steve, 'but at this stage we were just guessing at it, we hadn't realized how far behind the times our machine was. Although we'd converted the outfit to a kneeler, we hadn't moved the wheels in enough to compensate. That was just typical of the sort of errors we made. We spent a year copying club lads and not always the same club lads, and anything that seemed to work was tried on the Fidderman – it was a real hotch-potch. Our tuning was equally hit and miss as we threw more bits away than we put in. However, by 1980 we had got to grips with tuning and our Suzuki-engined hybrid seriously worried quite a few people.'

The Fidderman outfit had been supplied with a vertical twin 650cc Triumph engine and was of the front exit type, where the passenger sat on a bolted-on 'chair'. After their visits to the race tracks and 'chance' calls on local competitors, especially the well-known Andrews brothers in York, they had the opportunity to study the opposition's machines in much greater detail, and the basic format of their outfit began to evolve. A modern, water-cooled, three-cylinder two-stroke Suzuki engine and gearbox replaced the outdated Triumph unit. The old chassis was cut up and rewelded to make it into a 'kneeler' and the sidecar platform was extensively altered to become a rear exit type so that the passenger could lean further out to enhance cornering speeds. The rebuilding process took nearly a year to complete, the finished article bearing no resemblance to the humble machine which had spawned it. At this stage in his career, Steve had virtually no knowledge of the effects of weight distribution on handling and braking performance. The radically altered machine was to display some weird characteristics, but the enthusiastic twosome, with absolutely no previous experience, thought that all sidecars must handle like theirs!

All top teams know the value of testing and the Webster equipe was no exception. The reborn Fidderman was loaded on to a modified boat trailer and taken to Full Sutton airfield, near York. At first Mick took the outfit around the track, the eager lads taking it in turn to passenger. Although the brothers had spectated at many a meeting, they had no idea what it would feel like to be on a sidecar and neither of them enjoyed the experience. 'I can remember Dad bombed along,' says Steve 'and all I could think was, I hope he stops soon.' Mick was unaware that the boys were so unhappy. Steve could not get on with passengering but after a few laps Kevin could see that Steve did have a natural aptitude as the rider, and said that he was prepared to be passenger. The pairing worked well; they powered around Full Sutton and had got the 'circuit' worked out to a tee. 'Full Sutton had a long straight and a corner,' describes Steve; 'you could power along the straight and go right and then turn the outfit around and go the other way. We were brilliant. If they ever held a race at Full Sutton we'd win it hands down. What we weren't aware of is that real race tracks have different corners and varying gradients. We thought we were fantastic, but in reality we had a hell of a lot to learn!'

At long last the great day arrived, the day of the race. The Websters had experienced a sleepless night, every one too excited to relax. They were up at the crack of dawn; the bike loaded up and ready to go. The race was to be at Elvington, 30 miles away.

'We loaded up our trailer. It was spot on. We didn't know it, but at this period of our career we had the fastest transporter and the slowest bike! We had a 3-litre Capri and a modified boat trailer. My dad had modified the rear wheels of the trailer so that all the weight was over the back. It flew, which is more than you could say for the Fidderman!

'We were the first to arrive at Elvington. We tentatively walked the course, the race day butterflies stirring in our stomachs. Elvington is an airfield and so the track was not marked out until race day. You could get an idea of the line by walking the course.' But a surprise was in store for young Webster despite this advance inspection.

'I had a fair idea of the track from this early morning walkabout,' says Steve, 'left here, right there, long straight and so on. But, what you can see standing up and what you can see from a bike are two very different things. I set off and I was horrified! All I could see were cones, cones, cones. No trees, no signs, the gap for the pits barely visible. I knew roughly where each corner came but I couldn't judge distance. There were cones on either side of me but it was only when cones appeared in front of me that I realized this was the corner. Also, after a few races the cones moved due to being knocked about or moved for access to an incident, so the track changed subtly, and sometimes not so subtly as the day progressed. I hadn't realized at first that the cones could move and I'd have a corner worked out at a certain speed, and then arrive there to find the corner had changed shape and I couldn't go round it as fast as I thought. It was a nightmare!'

Mick had stressed the need to get a good start; he had instilled in the boys that 90 per cent of racing is the ability to get away well. Unlike Grand Prix racing, where the race is run over a distance of about 60 miles, the format at club level is to have three races during the day, each one lasting only four or five laps. If you didn't get a good start, there wasn't enough time to make up the lost ground in the few laps that the race lasted. He was so enthusiastic in labouring this point that he had totally omitted to say that the ability to stop is also a prerequisite of survival in the racing jungle.

'Talk about a good start,' glows Webster, 'we were off like the proverbial substance off a shovel. From a grid of about 12 machines we were at the back, where novices have to start. We made at least six places before the first corner, but when everyone started to brake for the corner, I rapidly discovered another shortcoming in our much modified machine – the brakes!' All the machines at the front of the grid had disc brake systems whereas the Websters' much older design had the far less efficient drum brakes. Being unable to slow down as quickly as the opposition Steve and Kevin were catapulted to the front of the field, mainly because the errant outfit ran into the back of one of the better braked leaders! The collision slowed Steve enough for him to get round the corner and eliminated one of the favourites with a flat rear tyre. Having survived the first corner chaos, which they had created, our debutants managed to complete the race. It must be said that although they were somewhat chastened by the 'outbraking' manouevre at the first corner, they did not slow down much and had several other incidents on the way to a third place finish.

At the end of the race Webster had certainly made a name for himself. The paddock was alive with news of the lunatic on the white outfit with a red stripe on it. No-one was more interested in the tales about this newcomer than the poor competitor, the eliminated favourite, who had had his rear tyre rudely removed at the first corner. He paced the paddock inquiring about the twosome's whereabouts. Webster made himself scarce, at the hot dog stand or having a nerve-settling coffee, conveniently out of the way. Steve tells us that it is an advantage nowadays not being instantly recognizable, and indeed it was also a real plus on this early occasion. 'At one point, this furious bloke came up to me with this shredded tyre in his hand. He asked if I seen the brainless b****rd who had a white bike, number 27 he thought. "Don't know him, pal", I nervously replied. I knew just how expensive tyres were, and I quickly motioned to my dad that we'd better be off. Dad is ever the optimist, and as we loaded up, he patted the Capri and said, "One thing, lad, once we're in this bugger, nothing will catch us!"'

So, Steve Webster left the scene of his first race. On the journey home the talk was of all the things which needed to be improved. 'All the testing at Full Sutton had stood us in good stead,' reflects Steve. 'We knew how to work together and drift the bike if we got a bit untidy. In a way we outrode ourselves and the equipment. The brakes, due to our modifications, caused the front wheel to go 'light' and the handling to desert us. We were using Dunlop Green Spot tyres, which were treaded, and all the other runners were on 13in slicks.' Although observers on that day would certainly have described the Webster duo as wild, the boys were blissfully unaware of their over exuberant youthful enthusiasm. 'We were in far too much of a rush,' remarks Steve. 'When I think back to those days, I think of it as my Championship dash. We were bound to come unstuck sooner or later. You really can't run before you can walk, but I didn't believe that at the time.' The learning curve in motorsport is steep and long, and the brothers were just beginning.

The pair had entered the Auto 66 round of races pretty late in the season. Although they were aware that the bike would need to be updated for the following season, they were keen to do as many races as they could in the remaining months. The series ran at Elvington and Carnaby. The second race was again at Elvington and was just as spectacular as its predecessor.

The first practice session passed without incident, if you discount a couple of harmless spins 'just finding the limit', according to Steve! Once again the brothers Webster heeded their father's advice and made a superb start. This time they got the braking right and were amongst the leaders at the end of the first lap. As the race progressed Steve and Kevin were challenging for the lead, and what their machine lacked in ability was more than made up for by the determination of its pilot. Unfortunately, in their enthusiasm the Websters were once again overdriving the outfit. Several times in their quest to grab the lead of the race, the pair overcooked it and were on the brink of having a major accident. Eventually the inevitable happened and Steve arrived at one of the corners far too quickly, exceeding the capabilities of the drum-braked device. 'There's a corner at Elvington,' recalls Steve 'where all the marshals congregate. They are usually watching the racing, but on this particular day something had distracted them and they were standing with their backs to the track. Kev and I came barrelling through, totally out of control, and missed the marshals by inches. They jumped in all directions and there was much fist shaking and shouting of expletives. We were losing valuable time and had to go the long way around to rejoin the race. We had cones jammed under the fairing but some creative manoeuvring soon dislodged them. Somehow or other we managed to get going again and finished first! We were really chuffed. I realized that the crowd shared our pride only for it to be shattered when a member of the Auto 66 club came up to me at the end of the race. I thought he'd come to congratulate us on our superb control! He said, "I bet you thought you'd won that, didn't you?" and, not detecting the hint of sarcasm in his voice, I cheerfully replied, "Yeah, yeah, it was good that". But then his face changed: "I think bloody good, you're a maniac, a nutter. You're barred, mate, now get off home. I'm doing you a favour barring you because if you carry on like that you'll bloody top yourself!".'

As usual in times of stress, Mick came to the rescue. Mick's years in racing had given him the ability to stand back and review a situation and deal with matters diplomatically. He told Steve to go and pack up while he went to talk to Pete Hillaby, the organizer of the Auto 66 club races. Pete understood that it was all boyish enthusiasm and said he agreed with the ban, but perhaps a one meeting ban would cool the lads' ardour. However, for that day the Webster racing was over.

Looking back on this, Steve admits the incident was his fault, but he insists that the marshals should have been watching the racing: 'I'm sure every marshal will agree that there are times when you have to be ready to run and take avoiding action. Marshals are there to prevent incidents, not be part of one!'

The next round was at Carnaby and Steve hoped that a change of venue might help with the hitherto accident prone run of luck, but alas, this was not the case. Carnaby was in fact the scene of the first major Webster racing crash, as Steve vividly recalls: 'We came out of the Esses at Carnaby and into the hairpin. Out of the hairpin there is a fast left-hander, then a straight, and then a sharp right-hander. By the time we arrived at the right-hander we were very much out of control! It was the usual situation of trying to keep up with the better bikes. We struggled round another lap and this time, at the left-hander out of the hairpin, we flipped it over. Kevin was thrown out of the outfit and yours truly went along, with the outfit on its side scraping the ground, until it hit the fence. This was an opportunity for the spectators who had parked near the fence to have a bit of first-hand involvement in sidecar action!

One moment they were sitting on their bonnets enjoying pie and peas, a Carnaby speciality, and hot coffee, the next, enter the Websters! I demolished part of the fence and pie, peas and coffee were everywhere! I've never seen people move their legs so fast. If they hadn't reacted quickly, crushed bones would have been added to our list of misdemeanours! Meanwhile, poor Kev was wandering around in the middle of the track, wondering where he was and suffering from concussion. Pete Hillaby was seriously concerned – but not for the sake of Kevin or myself; no, he was furious about the damage to the fence!'

Steve continues: 'This was typical of our first year in racing, a real wing and a prayer job! People who saw us in those early days would have thought that we were crackers – definitely. But it wasn't really like that. There are people who go racing and just being in a race is the end in itself. To us however, we had to be the best. We had to be the winners yesterday but we were in far too much of a hurry. We tried to make the bike do things it wasn't capable of. We were permanently on the limit.'

It wasn't only the crowds and the organizers that Webster impressed in those early days. There were other riders that he influenced quite strongly. 'There was one bloke who raced a real big outfit. It was Honda CBX-powered, a six-cylinder engine of great power and complexity. I just can't remember his name. He was always in the same bunch as us battling for the lead. Kev and I were always getting 'mixed up' in front of him and either Kevin would fall out or I'd get it wrong and we'd end up sideways. We were at about the same level, but somehow we always arrived at the corner first. We'd battle like mad with him – it was real hammer and tongs stuff – but he got so neurotic about us that he'd slow down and see what incident we were going to have. In the end he came to see me and said "Look, I'm giving up this sidecar racing, it's always you two spinning off in front of me. Good luck lads, but I can't take anymore, I'm packing it in".'

Problems had also come to a head around this time in Webster's personal life. Jill did not enjoy the racing and she certainly did not enjoy the disruption that it caused in the marital home. DIY was not Webster's forte and it got an even lower priority than usual if jobs on the bike were pressing. 'I think it was the final straw for Jill when the house had been covered in dust sheets for six months because I was working on the bike and I was supposed to be building a fireplace. I had made a start – two bricks were laid – but the bike was more of a challenge to me. One night, Jill was sitting there on a dust sheet-covered chair, watching the telly, which was balanced on a bike wheel! Suddenly she got up and attacked the bike with a sweeping brush. We were too young to be tied down and I must have been impossible to put up with. We went our separate ways but are still good friends.'

At the end of the 1979 season the brothers took stock of their situation. They had competed in six events, their one win had been denied them, but they had survived relatively unscathed despite numerous spins and several fairly large accidents. They knew that their home-brewed machine was uncompetitive; the engine was reasonably powerful, but the chassis, brakes and tyres were not up to the job. They had learned a great deal from their brief career so far, although they still had difficulty in understanding the roles that each of them had to play. They were still very inexperienced and had only taken the first rung on the ladder to success.

For the 1980 season a newer, but not new, Derbyshire chassis was bought. Miraculously they managed to sell the hacked-about Fidderman, and with help from Dad they fitted the three-cylinder Suzuki engine into the new machine. The Derbyshire was, and is, a popular and competitive conventional tubular-steel short-chassis outfit, favoured by clubmen racers for its simple design and predictable handling characteristics. Steve was convinced that armed with a competitive chassis and their powerful Suzuki engine, he and Kevin had a very good chance of winning the Auto 66 Club Championship.

The plan for 1980 was to contest all the rounds of the Auto 66 series and to take in other events at more distant circuits which did not clash with their prime objective of winning the Club Championship.

Although the Derbyshire chassis was a much better prospect than the hybrid Fidderman, their results remained inconsistent because they were still at the bottom of a very steep learning curve and continued to be erratic in their riding style. Many observers were of the opinion that the young Webster brothers were wild men and that their participation in the sport would be terminated very quickly, either because of a massive accident, or by the intervention of officialdom on the grounds that they were a menace to themselves and everyone else! One seasoned reporter described their efforts as 'an accident looking for somewhere to happen'. Steve is adamant that they were not wild, merely in far too much of a hurry to get to the top, and that they could not see that in order to go quicker they needed to steady down a little.

The 1980 season progressed in much the same vein as its predecessor; flashes of blinding speed punctuated by numerous spins and accidents. Steve admits that he 'lost' Kevin on numerous occasions mainly because they were trying too hard. The biggest problem facing the accident prone duo was a complete lack of understanding of the other's role and contribution. Steve says, 'I had only been on the chair for a few runs round Full Sutton and did not understand what it was like at racing speeds and under racing conditions. I used to say to Kev, "if you lean out a bit further on that corner, we can get round it much quicker". Kev would just look at me as if to say, "What do you know?" Then he would lean out further and either I'd spin it or Kev would fall out, or we'd turn over!' They tried to discuss their respective contributions but the basic lack of understanding and their relative inexperience led to arguments and accidents. Eventually they gave up trying to analyze each other's efforts; Kevin said, "Just go as fast as you can and I'll hang on."

In an effort to increase the speed of their outfit, the road-going Suzuki GT750 engine was tuned, but yet again their inexperience showed through. The dominant engine at this time was the four-cylinder two-stroke Yamaha, a 700cc version of the Grand Prix racing engine, rather than a converted road engine. In an effort to match the Yamahas and the bigger capacity four-stroke engines, Steve tuned his three-cylinder Suzuki to give it more top-end power. In so doing he destroyed the flexibility of the engine, giving it a very narrow power band and making it much more difficult to drive. In comparison with their much more experienced opposition, Steve and Kevin had a machine with a very sudden delivery of power so it was all or nothing, meaning that they had to get through the corners very quickly to keep the revs up, which led to the inevitable accidents.

During the 1980 season Steve and Kevin ventured further afield, taking in races at Croft, Cadwell Park, Mallory Park,

Donington and Knockhill in addition to the Auto 66 races at Carnaby and Elvington. Steve remembers Donington particularly because it was so different from the circuits where they were used to racing: 'Donington was wonderful, the facilities were so good, the track surface was like a billiard table compared with the bumpy club circuits that we were used to.'

The pair had obviously got a lot of talent; they were keeping up with, and often beating, much more experienced crews on better machinery. The fact that they were having to try too hard was a result of inexperience and inferior equipment, rather than a basic desire to self-destruct!

Towards the end of 1980, a chance meeting with an enthusiastic spectator at the Knockhill circuit in Scotland was to have a dramatic effect on Steve's career.

5

Making Progress

Mick was leaning on the fence at the rural Scottish circuit of
Knockhill, watching his offspring power round in their newly
renovated Derbyshire outfit. A new colour scheme had been
chosen for the bodywork to make it more eyecatching; the fairing
was white with a bold red stripe on it, and to give the design
more definition a black line had been painted in, to make the red
stand out.

Another spectator joined Mick, and to Mick's delight
commented on the outfit. 'Looks very smart, are they your lads?'
inquired the stranger. 'That's right,' answered Mick proudly.
'They seem to be doing quite well,' continued the bloke, studying
the race results from previous outings that were listed in the back
of his programme. 'Not bad considering their budget,' elaborated
Mick, 'but what we really need is one of those elusive Yamaha
engines, but that's out I'm afraid.'

The companion went on to ask Mick why they'd chosen those
particular colours for the sidecar. Mick confessed there was no
special reason except that they looked smart and that the team
were keen to give a professional image, especially as they were
seeking sponsors.

The man then went on to introduce himself: 'I'm Paul Seward
and I have a string of outlets for agricultural machinery. Those
colours on your outfit happen to be International Harvester's
colours. I'm here watching my lad race solos and those colours
caught my eye.'

The new friendship between Mick and Paul Seward progressed
over the two-day meeting and by the end of the weekend Paul had

offered to give the Webster team a helping hand. He recognized the talent displayed by Steve and Kevin and would help them all he could.

Mick had outlined their financial struggle and Paul was impressed by how far they'd come on a shoestring budget. He bought them the Yamaha engine that they were dreaming of and asked that they return it to him at the end of the season. This stranger who casually chatted to Mick at Knockhill effectively changed Steve's life. 'If there's one bloke who put me where I am today,' says the four times World Champion, 'it's Paul Seward. He opened all the doors for me and I know that without him I would never have achieved so much.'

Paul brought a more professional image to the team; he produced press releases and issued other interested parties with handouts and championship standing tables. He wrote to other companies with early portfolios trying to recruit other sponsors.

To complement their new motive power a Windle chassis was bought, the Derbyshire chassis and Suzuki engine being sold to finance the purchase. The Windle outfit was considered to be the best of its kind, a conventional tubular short chassis built by Terry Windle at Thurgoland, a small village in the hills above Sheffield. Terry Windle has a reputation for being a meticulous engineer, his products being beautifully crafted and assembled, with the attention to detail that is a hallmark of the true professional. The short-chassis Windle has been in the forefront of British sidecar racing for over a decade, although Terry's later efforts with an LCR-type, long-wheelbase machine have been less successful.

For the first time in his short career, Steve had the equipment to complement his speed and aggression. He was still short on experience and in too much of a rush to get to the top, but at least he could now compete on equal terms.

The 1981 season saw Steve and Kevin consolidate their raw speed into tangible results. At every meeting they were contesting the lead, and were front runners in the Auto 66 Club Championship. They were very difficult to beat at Elvington and Carnaby, their local circuits, although usually beating themselves by trying too hard and having spins and accidents, but many race wins were notched up as well. The season produced some memorable dices, their main opposition being the outfits of Chas

Greatorix, Mick Hudson and Mick Stearno, all experienced competitors. The young upstarts were capable of running with the very best, often humbling much more experienced crews as their knowledge and experience began to complement their outright pace. In addition to the Auto 66 Championship they also travelled further afield gaining experience at different circuits. They contested New Era and Bemsee meetings at circuits as far away as Thruxton in Hampshire, Brands Hatch in Kent and Snetterton in Norfolk. Despite not being able to indulge themselves in private testing at these remote venues, the Websters were on the pace wherever they went, learning new circuits quickly and making a reputation for themselves as the hottest prospects on the sidecar scene.

Although they were beginning to get results, the pairing could not shake off the tag of wild men. They were still having far too many accidents as they pushed themselves beyond the limits of their meagre experience. 'I was terrible with the throttle,' admits Steve. 'I just did not appreciate that a passenger cannot react as quickly as I could; I forgot he had to manoeuvre his body weight whereas all my decisions were mental and involved a flick of the wrist or a kick of a pedal. I was not accommodating to passengers at all.'

Along with increased Championship aspirations came the opportunity to travel further afield and visit different circuits. Those who think motorsport is a glamorous life have never had the dubious pleasure of camping at various circuits in a variety of weather conditions in economy class accommodation. Although Steve and Kevin could now afford to spread their wings a little and go further than Elvington, they could not afford a caravan or motorhome. So, overnight lodging was provided by a large but aged frame tent. Early in the season the duo decided to contest a round at Snetterton, Norfolk. Although the journey would take a good five hours, the team could not set off until 5 o'clock as everyone had to clock-off from their day jobs. The journey to Snetterton from Yorkshire is most unpleasant as the A17 carries many heavy lorries, and in the dark, after a day at Rowntrees, it requires a lot of concentration. Having made it as far as King's Lynn by 10 o'clock, the team decided to stop at a welcoming hostelry to break the journey. Whilst Ray Lund, their co-opted mechanic, downed the orange juices, as he was suddenly the driver, the brothers sampled the Wethereds bitter. A couple of hours later, the trio set off on their merry way to Snetterton.

In those days, Snetterton in the spring was a marvellous place: wind howling, and a paddock made of compressed mud with very few facilities. In the pitch blackness our team was trying to erect their huge frame tent. The rain was pouring down and Ray was getting less and less amused by the giggling Webster boys as they tried to assemble their accommodation. 'Every time we pushed a tent pole in the ground, it slowly keeled over as everywhere was so muddy,' remembers Steve. 'In the end we just threw the canvas on the ground and crawled in it. The next morning the other teams emerged from their caravans and properly assembled tents and looked in amazement as we three crawled out of a muddy tarpaulin. "Morning pal", I said to a transfixed onlooker, "I see it's stopped raining then!"'

By the time the team visited Donington later in the season they had been upgraded and had a bus to sleep in provided by Paul Seward. Knowing that they did not need to worry about making camp, the team plus several 'helpers' – lads who had come along to be gofers – nearing Donington, headed not for a prime spot in the paddock but to the nearest pub which had a disco!

The Paul Seward bus was parked in the pub car park and the lads went off in search of local talent. Their mission a failure, but consoled by several pints, the entourage eventually decided that they may as well head for the circuit. They weaved back to the coach to find it totally blocked in by cars. It was obvious why their pulling power had been so limited when they saw the calibre of car surrounding their vehicle: Jaguars, Mercedes and even the occasional Rolls. Webster, elected spokesman, was sent back into the pub armed with a list of registrations asking for the owners to move their cars. The owners were obviously busy with more pressing matters and not one of them came to the aid of the team.

'Only one thing for it, then,' decided Steve, 'there's plenty of us, we'll lift the cars out of the way and clear a space.' After an hour of frantic activity the car park was rearranged and the bus made its escape.

With the season nearing its end Steve and Kevin headed for Carnaby and the final round of the Auto 66 Championship. They had had a marvellous season with their on-track successes coupled with many off-track escapades; they had learned a great deal and had matured considerably, at least as sidecar racers! At the final round of the Club Championship they only needed to pick up a handful of points to clinch the title. They worked out that one fifth place finish from the three races that afternoon would guarantee them the title. They knew that they could take it easy and that there was no pressure on them to win because they had a very healthy lead in the points standings. Their main rival was Mick Hudson, who would have to win all three races, with the Websters failing to finish higher than sixth in any race to beat them. With this in mind you would expect the brothers to have taken it gently to ensure their first Championship victory. This, however, was not their way; they only knew how to go flat-out!

Having made their customary good start, Steve and Kevin were contesting the lead with Mick Hudson and Chas Greatorix. Although they knew that they only had to finish where they were, their natural exuberance got the better of them and they started to push for the lead. At the end of the start-and-finish straight at Carnaby is a long, double-apex right-hand bend which leads to a left–right–left chicane. This combination puts a tremendous strain on the passenger: he needs to be firmly over the back wheel on the long right-hander, quickly transferring his weight to the left as the machine starts to change direction. To go through the chicane quickly and smoothly requires the passenger to make four major changes of position on the bike in a very short space of time. To make this possible it is helpful if the driver is smooth with the throttle and brake, as any violent change, such as braking or accelerating whilst the passenger is changing position, can cause him to lose his grip and fall off. In his haste to take the lead Steve went into the chicane just a little too quickly. Suddenly he had to grab at the brakes to make sure that they got around the corner, and this unsettled the machine. To make matters even worse, Steve then opened the throttle fully. Not wishing to lose any ground to his competitors, he thought he would make up for his error on the brakes by getting back on the power earlier than the other outfits. However, the net effect of this sudden deceleration followed by the equally violent application of power whilst the machine was going from right lock to left lock and back to right lock, was to make the machine 'flick' out of line. This 'flick' was so vicious that Kevin was thrown off the machine, which was travelling at about 90mph. Steve, meanwhile, realized that he had lost his brother but was fighting to bring the out-of-control device to a standstill.

As soon as the machine came to a halt, Steve quickly dismounted and ran to his brother's aid. The marshals had rushed to attend immediately and Kevin was lifted to the safety of a field adjoining the track whilst the ambulance was sent for.

'I could see that Kevin's leg was badly broken,' Steve recalls. 'The top half of his leg was pointing to the side and bone was piercing the skin. I felt really guilty. Kev had always said: "Don't bother about me, just go faster". Now, I'd been instrumental in doing this to my own brother. Poor Kev, he was an innocent victim of my charge to the top. I was busy worrying about all this when I heard Kevin say: "Get another passenger for the last race, make sure we win the Championship, then we'll at least have something". So, I had to pull myself together and get organized. As Kev was lifted into the ambulance he called out again, "Get someone on, Steve, and win that trophy".'

Although Steve didn't really feel like battling on, he knew he had to try and finish what he and Kevin had striven for all season. He went around the paddock looking for a passenger. Eddy Wright suggested a bloke from their team and hasty introductions were made and a stand-in recruited.

The second race was used as a practice session for the Kevin replacement to get used to the bike and to Steve. All went well and the pair finished midfield.

'I asked this guy if he felt comfortable, and he assured me he did,' Steve informs us. 'I was so upset and worried I can't even remember this poor bloke's name, though I'm sure he'll remember the race! We got off to a good start and my customary red haze soon took over and it wasn't long before I was battling with Chas Greatorix, Mick Stearno and Mick Hudson. I'd forgotten this wasn't Kev in the chair. The poor bloke was totally out of synchronization with me, as at this time, Kevin was the only person on earth who could ride with me, but I didn't realize this until many years later. He was thrown about as if he was on a bucking bronco; he grabbed my foot instead of the handle and was getting in the way as I tried to change gear. We finished in the top five and the Championship was mine and Kev's. One of my stand-in passenger's friends rushed up to congratulate him. "Hey, you did well there, son", he said, but my passenger did not want to chat, "Let me get out of here" he seethed, "and away from HIM, Steve Webster, he's f***ing mad!"'

With a pedigree such as that it was going to be hard for Steve to find a replacement for Kevin whilst he recuperated. Kevin's initial joy, as Steve bounded into the hospital with the news that they were the 1981 Auto 66 Club Champions, soon turned to despair when he was told by the doctors that his femur was so badly fractured that he would need an operation to insert a steel pin and many months of physiotherapy. Naturally, all Kevin wanted to know was when could he ride again, and was told such pursuits wouldn't be possible for many many months, if ever. Such strain on his leg, even when he recovered, was not advisable. For Kevin Webster it felt as if the bottom had just fallen out of his world.

It was another situation of 'what next' for the Webster team. Steve was still riddled with guilt that he had caused the accident. 'Even to this day,' says Steve, 'I know that I was partly to blame for Kevin's accident. I had a total lack of understanding about the role of the passenger.'

After much heart searching and discussion it was agreed that Steve must carry on and that what happened with Kevin's prospects would have to be reviewed when he was fully fit. Many people had begun to notice the talent of the Webster boys and potential sponsors were taking an interest.

So, who could replace Kevin? Many passengers were in awe of Steve, feeling he was too hot to handle. He rang a lot of people in his search for a passenger, but there was hardly a queue of willing encumbants. Eventually, Steve rang John Evans, a local rider, and he suggested Tony Hewitt. Hewitt had been passengering for 14 years and was in fact toying with retiring. He was a 30-year-old British Rail employee with a wife and young family. He had a very good reputation as an excellent passenger, and although Steve admits he hadn't heard of Tony he gave him a call. However, Hewitt was not particularly enthusiastic about joining Steve. 'Well,' he said 'see how it goes, and if you're stuck for Brands give me a buzz.'

Steve did not follow up this offer as he could tell Hewitt was not really keen. Meanwhile, a local lad called Fisher offered to partner Steve. Webster and Fisher had their one and only outing at Brands Hatch, but the pair could not get on at all. Steve was so accustomed to the long-suffering Kevin that he thought Fisher very critical. The fact that Webster spun at Paddock Bend and tipped young Fisher out confirmed in Fisher's mind the rumours he had heard about Steve. Kevin had moulded himself to compensate for Steve's overtly aggressive style and other mortals were not going to be able to do this. A refining of the Webster style was seriously needed, but someone had to be found who could do it.

A further two months trickled by and the Webster career had come to a standstill. Given a clean bill of health after breaking his wrist during a night out with friends, Steve contacted Tony again as the 1982 season was about to begin. The pair, for one reason and another, had missed the winter test sessions, and with no time to test and both riders having full-time employment to consider as well as racing, it was agreed that Webster and Hewitt should enter a race at Snetterton.

Steve was delighted with Hewitt's performance but Hewitt had to tell Steve a few home truths. 'You're far too erratic, lad. All this on and off the power arrangement is scrubbing speed off. You've got to learn to be smooth,' Hewitt protested.

'I owe such a lot to Tony,' says Steve, 'he really developed my riding style. At first I was shocked that he dare tell me how to ride. I was an arrogant little person having won the Auto 66 Championship, but I take my hat off to Tony. He laid down the law to me at a formative time in my career. He made me listen to him, and gradually our results improved.'

Webster often found it hard to implement Hewitt's ideas about driving style. Steve is a very aggressive rider and Tony laboured away at trying to make him smoother.

'I found it really hard to conform,' confesses Steve. 'Tony was always telling me off. Once, in the wet, I'd chucked him out through being too rough and he told me in the paddock afterwards that he knew I would do it – I always did that in the wet. Of course he was right, but I didn't always appreciate the post-race analysis!'

Whether or not Tony Hewitt found Steve an irresistible

challenge may never be known, but he did agree to passenger the rebel for no more than two years, and then he would retire. He had a formidable task ahead of him taming the young hotshoe.

However, Tony Hewitt's hard work paid off in the end. He was a key figure in Webster's journey on the learning curve. He was the man who slowed down Webster's rush a little and instilled quality and consistency into the partnership.

During 1982 our new pairing contested the Marlborough Clubman's Championship. They won most races, and if they came in second, the winners were Darren Dixon and Terry McGahan. The battle for the Championship went right to the last round at Silverstone. 'I think this was a psychological victory, sooner than one based on talent', reminisces Steve. 'It turned wet just before the race. We had our wet tyres on and my dad had employed one of his demon tweeks, picked up during his grasstrack racing years. He had taped polythene all around the fairing and the mudguard to cut down on the amount of spray. Darren spotted this in the assembly area and quickly tried to do the same to his outfit. Doing this in a rush, he made a mess of it, and throughout the race, plastic and tape were flapping everywhere. He came in fourth from last, his worst result all season. Darren had gone to pieces in this last minute rush and the Championship was ours!'

Another victory in 1982 came in the Southern 100 race in the Isle of Man, where Webster and Hewitt set the lap record, which remained uncontested for seven years until it was beaten in 1989. 'Thinking back to the Southern 100 race makes me shiver,' states Steve. 'I was so reckless then. I had no idea of my own mortality whatsoever. There's a place called the Bombhole where you go between two kerbs, and when you come out you hit a manhole cover. I didn't ease off for this and every time we went over the manhole, the bike went into a massive wobble. How we stayed on the bike I just don't know. We were like two rag dolls. This race was our first road race and it was a real wing and a prayer job. We were dicing with Tony Baker and how we coped remains a mystery. I wouldn't like to think I'd got to do it now. I am so much more aware of danger. I must be getting old!'

All through 1982 Webster and Hewitt had been courting the attention of Dennis Trollope, who dealt in parts for bikes. He was involved with Fowlers of Bristol, but did not work for them.

Rumour had it that Dennis was keen to sponsor a sidecar outfit again. He had been very involved in sponsoring the late Jock Taylor, and after Jock's untimely death Dennis had withdrawn his interest from the sport for a while. Dennis was undecided whether to invest in Steve and Tony or in the Folkestone pairing of brothers Darren and Sean Dixon. Dennis had been attending many meetings up and down the country and was often greeted by the faces of Webster and Hewitt openly pestering to be sponsored.

'We were getting like two fractious kids,' remarks Steve, 'hanging round Trollope's van saying, "Will you back us? Go on, please, are you going to?" We had long since given up being subtle.

'I don't even know if the Dixons know this,' reveals Steve, 'but there were only the two of us in the equation. Dennis had almost decided to back Darren and Sean, and he went along to Brands Hatch for a final look. It's funny how things happen in life, and it's often true that small things swing the course of events. That's certainly what happened in this case, for on the day that Dennis was on his 'make your mind up' visit to Brands, the Dixons had a puncture. Like us, they were operating on a limited budget and just could not afford to put a new tyre on the outfit. In order to keep going they persistently pumped the tyre up. We've all done things like this, but in Dennis' eyes it was lack of preparation, so he decided to back us. All I could say was, "The party's at Flawith!" It was a major break for us.'

Dennis Trollope demanded a lot in terms of commitment from the pair: smoking and drinking were out and female friends hanging around at the circuit were definitely not on. 'Dennis has an absolute dislike of smoking,' says Webster. 'I've a collection of anoraks with burned pockets where a crafty fag has been hastily stuffed as Dennis has approached.' Steve even broke off courting his wife Karen to comply with Dennis' regime, but happily they did reunite!

So the Webster operation still had the on-going support from Paul Seward and now had extra backing from Dennis Trollope. Dennis Trollope also fixed up the Silkolene sponsorship which Webster has to this day. The pair owned a short-based Windle chassis and a Yamaha 750cc engine, paid for by Mick and Paul Seward, but Dennis did not wish them to use that outfit; he wanted to assume control.

'The deal with Dennis was like this,' explains Steve. 'Dennis would supply everything, bike, engine, carburettors, parts, everything. In return, we were to give him 50 per cent of our winnings. This was a gift of a deal – all that support for half a trophy. We had it made. I really needed this chance to show people what I was capable of.'

However, Webster was not going to have it all his own way. Dennis Trollope was keen for Webster and Hewitt to use the long-wheelbase Windle chassis; in fact the same that Jock Taylor had been using at the time of his fatal accident, albeit repaired and extensively overhauled. Dennis was also specific about the choice of engine. He did not want Steve to use his own 750 Yamaha, but either a 500 Yamaha or a 700 Yamaha. Steve was not too pleased about this stipulation as he knew his 750 Yamaha would be faster, but Dennis had a master plan. Forces were afoot in the shape of Hewitt and Dennis Trollope to slow Webster down a bit in order to teach him some racecraft, especially considering Webster's lack of formal racing credentials: he and Kevin had jumped on the outfit and tried their damnedest, but there comes a time when one has to refine one's style, and this for Webster was it. He found it most frustrating!!

'I knew I needed Dennis. There was no way I could finance this step on the ladder myself, but I knew I was being held back,' complains Steve. It was only years later that he fully understood what Dennis Trollope was trying to do. He did hold Webster back; he wanted him to struggle with his down-on-power engines and that way, learn to ride. With lots of horsepower, Steve would have blasted off into the lead risking the lives of Hewitt and himself. Now was a time when the learning curve levelled out. Steve was madly frustrated; he was being beaten by Keith Cousins on a conventional bike and he hated the long-wheelbase Windle. 'Dennis was very experienced at running all sorts of engines. I was sure this must all be doing me good but it was very hard to swallow,' comments Steve.

The bike handled appallingly, and both Steve and Tony were concerned about their safety. 'Sometimes the beast would pull to the left and so you'd say to yourself, "right, next time on that bend I'll compensate". You'd arrive at the same curve and the damn thing would go right. It was so unpredictable.'

The long-based Windle met its Waterloo at the 1983 TT races on the Isle of Man. Neither Steve nor Tony wanted to go to the Island, but it was a means to an end. The pair were keen to get into GP racing, but the route to that is usually via the European rounds. Dennis had done a deal with the ACU that if Tony and Steve did the TT, they would qualify for a GP start, missing out the need for European experience.

'We had been outpowered everywhere on this outfit,' recounts Steve, 'and at the TT it was handling badly as usual. We went off at the 13th Milestone in the race, and both ended up in hospital. I had neck injuries and Tony had back injuries. We felt fortunate to be alive. The TT has claimed so many lives. The biggest plus was that the long-based Windle had been written off. A blessing in disguise.'

Once they had recovered from their injuries sustained at the TT, Webster and Hewitt went on to complete the season on their own short-wheelbase Windle, using Dennis Trollope's 500 engine. Dennis had made the pair use this engine throughout the season, though they were not happy because the 700 and 750 engines had more torque, but Dennis was getting the pair used to the engine that he knew they would have to use in Grands Prix. 'I know now Dennis Trollope is a very wise, very experienced man,' comments Steve, 'but at the time I wanted to scream!' However, the experience and knowledge paid dividends.

The pair began to perform exceedingly well and entered the British Grand Prix at Silverstone.

'We went testing, and what Dennis told me to do with the engine somewhat shocked me,' recounts Steve. 'He said that he wanted me to rev the engine as far as it would go – just rev it and rev it until it blew up. This amazed me. I can remember asking Dennis if he really meant this; if I was misunderstanding him, I wanted to be sure. He couldn't really be saying, "Go out there and destroy an engine".' Yet, this is just what Dennis wanted Steve to do, in order to find the limit of the engine so that he knew how far to push the race unit. Sure enough, Steve complied with the instructions and Dennis, knowing the capacity of the rev band, stayed up all night and built another engine for race day.

'My head was full of facts and figures about the performance of other competitors,' recalls Steve, 'I'd seen Rolf Biland's times from Cadwell and I knew we were a good 10 seconds off his pace there. We were hopeful, however, that our short-based outfit would handle better at Silverstone than the long-wheelbased outfits. Although it sounds contradictory, the short outfits are better at long sweeping circuits such as Silverstone and the long ones seem to do well at tight, twisty circuits like Cadwell.'

Webster and Hewitt powered the outfit to finish fifth in the British GP and as arranged, handed over half of their prize money to Dennis. He showed his faith in the pair by immmediately handing this cash to the man who would drive the truck to the next GP in Sweden and said to our elated duo, 'I hope you've got enough holiday from work left. You're going to Sweden.'

So, with barely time to take in what was happening, Steve and Tony set off for Sweden. Unfortunately, despite very promising times in testing, they spun off in the race, only finishing a disappointing 14th after rejoining. Dennis was sufficiently impressed and instructed Webster and Hewitt to follow the Grand Prix circus to Mugello for the Italian Grand Prix. The pair tried hard as usual, but were thwarted by mechanical problems and did not finish here, realizing that to be competitive at GP level they needed an LCR.

For those unfamiliar with this term, LCR is short for Louis Christian Racing, the Swiss-based company that provides the majority of Grand Prix outfits. In conjunction with Rolf Biland, Louis Christian built the first long-wheelbase sidecar outfit. At the time of its introduction it was a radical departure from the conventional chassis in general use. Not only was the LCR considerably longer in the wheelbase, it was also constructed in a totally different manner from all the other contemporary chassis. The traditional method of chassis construction was to cut, bend and weld together tubular steel to form a framework upon which was mounted the engine, steering and suspension components. The LCR, however, borrowed heavily from car racing practice, using a lightweight aluminium monocoque backbone which incorporated an extension for the sidecar wheel. The suspension was radically different as well: the front suspension and steering was a trapezium consisting of unequal-length wishbones and pushrod actuation of the inboard spring damper unit, but the original and highly sophisticated steering system had to be modified when the FIM declared it to be illegal. The rear suspension also had its combined spring and damper unit located within the monocoque, operating a lower wishbone and upper transverse link through a system of bell cranks and pushrods. The sidecar wheel does not have any suspension, but is adjustable for ride height and for tracking and it is possible to move the third wheel in a fore-and-aft plane to alter the handling characteristics of the machine. All three wheels are fitted with powerful disc brakes.

The LCR 'worms', as they became known, offered a considerable performance benefit over conventional chassis. Because of their longer wheelbase, greater torsional rigidity and lighter weight, they were much faster through medium and high-speed corners. If they had a disadvantage, it was that they could not turn as sharply on low-speed bends as a short chassis could; they were also affected more by very bumpy circuits, but overall their advantage was so great that they revolutionized sidecar racing.

So huge is their superiority that LCRs have been unashamedly copied by other chassis builders. It must be said, though, that no-one has yet built a long chassis that can beat an LCR, and some efforts at 'improving' on Louis Christian's original have proved to be desperately lacking!

One of these copies was by a French gentleman who went by the name of Seymaz. Unfortunately, his copy of the LCR was not 'the same as' an LCR – indeed it was distinctly lacking. When LCR was mentioned to Dennis Trollope, he told Steve that he had purchased a Seymaz for Jock and it was a white elephant. This had completely put Dennis off any foreign chassis, and the dicing duo were to settle for a Windle or nothing.

Webster was convinced that the LCR was the key to success and he asked Paul Seward if anything could be done to acquire one. Paul could not help Steve singlehandedly, but said he would certainly make overtures to other potential sponsors.

Steve had not the maturity or clarity of thought at the time to think carefully about whether his obsession with having an LCR was really so important that he could afford to lose the support of Dennis Trollope. But he was young and impetuous, and Dennis was pushed aside, despite all he'd done, in Webster's single-minded dash to the Championship podium.

Steve waited and waited, the Windle offer from Dennis was still there, but he longed for an LCR. His heart leapt when Paul rang and said, 'About that chassis, there is a way we can get one.'

6

Taking on the World

Steve dashed down to Paul's place in Bishopthorpe to find out exactly what the deal entailed. It transpired that Paul had been talking to Peter Padgett, owner of Padgetts of Batley, a firm which sells Yamaha cycles and cycle parts. Peter had helped many young hopefuls on their way up the sporting ladder and was interested in Webster and Hewitt. Peter Padgett was willing to supply the pair with two race specification engines and to maintain them. This left Paul Seward's finances free to pay for the elusive chassis. He knew he had some money in the pot for his racing proteges, but he could not afford the chassis and engines as well. The deal was not without conditions: Steve and Tony were to pay 50 per cent of any prize money to the Padgett concern plus 50 per cent of any other sponsorship that they attracted. The bike would, of course, be in Padgett colours, carrying their name. This is quite usual in motorsport; the Padgetts were not greedy, just protecting their interests as well as enabling Steve to continue racing.

'I was hoping for help from a sponsor who would say "Go off, do your racing, let us know the costs and we'll come along to the meetings and we'll take on the world as a team",' says Steve. 'It was years later when I realized Dennis Trollope was the closest I'd ever get to this. He was an angel and I hadn't appreciated it.'

Hence, the Padgetts, although not fulfilling Steve's every requirement in his search for the perfect sponsor, gave him the chance to get the hallowed LCR. 'What seemed a wonderful opportunity,' recalls Steve 'was the biggest hiccup in my career.'

Webster quickly got to know other competitors who had taken the Padgett route: Mick Grant, Jon Eckerold, Steve Abbott and

Dennis and Julie Bingham. They were all happy with the help and support that Peter and his family gave them. 'Looking back,' philosophizes Steve, 'the others at that time of the day were just thrilled to be out there. I wanted to win, and that was where the difficulty lay.'

It wasn't long before it became plain to Steve that the assistance the Padgetts were willing to give was more in the role of patron than in the shape of World Championship sponsor. They had their business to run and there were other racers to help apart from the confident and eager Webster. It was a confusion of expectations – the Padgetts had one idea, Steve had another!

One area of discontent for Steve was the low priority that his engine appeared to be given. 'I remember preparing for the German Grand Prix in 1984,' he recollects. 'I had taken the engine down to Padgetts on the Saturday before I set sail on the Thursday morning. I was told this was ample time to get the engine rebuilt and to go to collect it on Wednesday lunchtime. When I arrived on Wednesday, I was horrifed to see Clive Padgett, son of Peter and excellent at his job of engine building, taking the engine out of its box. I inquired if it would be ready. "Oh yes", replied Clive, "but really I have more important things to do. For instance, I've got to clean the vans, we are due at Oulton Park testing tomorrow." I soon clicked that it might be prudent to offer to help so I volunteered to clean the vans, and was a bit cheesed off when the Padgett family also popped along with a couple of extra vans for me to do, but you can't have everything, as I'm always being told!'

However, Webster's attempt at becoming a car valet was shortlived, as Gary Padgett did not think the vans were pristine enough and criticized Steve's efforts. 'These vans are only half done', he said 'it would be different if we only half did your engine.''At first,' says Steve, 'I thought Gary was joking, then I realized this was sarcasm. So I picked up the engine and left. It was all in bits, but you can only push a Webster so far!'

'We worked all night on the engine, my dad and I. I suppose I didn't understand what the world of racing was really like. I had a lot of growing up to do,' Steve muses.

In fact during 1984, Steve Webster learned a lot about the racing world. One new discipline that he had to come to terms with was the amount of travelling involved in contesting both the British Championship and National and International events as well as the World Championship. The British Championship was relatively easy to co-ordinate as it was run over two days at Oulton Park and sponsored at that time by Marshall tractors. Travel around Britain proved easy, but their forays into the Grand Prix travelling circus give rise to many memories. 'This is going to make me look a real fool,' admits Steve, 'but when we first started racing abroad, we had no idea how to work out a route. If we were going to the Nurburgring, we'd go Dover, Calais, Ghent, Brussels, Aachen, Cologne! We'd actually get off the motorway, go through each place that we'd pinpointed on the map and then rejoin the motorway. Obviously we could bypass these places, but we just hadn't the experience of working out a route. It took us hours to get through Belgium!'

If a Padgett-loaned vehicle was not used, the Webster team would use a converted CF ambulance and often tow a caravan and trailer behind. 'This van was like Dr Who's tardis,' relates Webster. 'People were constantly amazed by what we could pack into it. Very often lots of helpers travelled with us. We used to break down frequently. Mostly we'd break down at least once on our way to pick up Tony from his place of work in Doncaster. On one journey we broke down on the way to get Tony and again in France; my dad was pushing the caravan and he pushed the back window in. By the end of the weekend the van was a mass of racer tape and temporary hoses, and the back window of the caravan was held in by stickers!'

Another occasion could have led to a massive road accident. The family Webster were progressing up the A1 after a race meeting when Steve noticed that the lights on the caravan didn't seem to be working. 'Go and waggle the lead', he instructed Karen. Karen, half asleep from a hectic race weekend, went round the back of the van and vaguely peered around. 'I couldn't believe it,' said Karen 'it just wasn't there and because I couldn't believe it, I started to look around to see if it had somehow rolled under the van!' 'What's going on?' snapped Steve, anxious to be home and incredulous that it was taking Karen so long to do a simple job. 'It's gone!' giggled Karen. She just couldn't imagine how you could lose a caravan. 'Well, it's like saying you've lost an elephant,' she remarks. 'Caravans are not exactly small things, you don't just misplace them.'

Steve was tired and now panic stricken. 'All I could visualize was this caravan rolling away down the A1 causing havoc. As we retraced our journey, I expected to see blue flashing lights at any minute and a trail of carnage all over the carriageways.'

The team retraced their steps to a hostelry called 'The Fox' just beside the A1, and there, waiting patiently, by the side of the road near a roundabout, not having caused a major road traffic accident, was the errant caravan. 'How lucky we were,' sighs Steve. It had come unhooked at slow speed and had stayed put.

On another occasion the Webster transporter was an uninvited bit part extra in a German movie! Steve and Tony were on their way back from Hockenheim. It was Tony's turn to drive and Steve was asleep in the back of the van. Suddenly, Steve was aware that he was surrounded by very bright lights. He peeped out of the window and saw a 1930s Rolls-Royce sail by. 'I was even more surprised when I saw lots of people in 1930s costumes,' remembers Steve. Meanwhile, Tony was being surprised by an irate director, who did *not* want a large van bearing the message WORLD CHAMPIONSHIP SIDECAR TEAM in the middle of his sensitive 1930s romance. 'Shift it, it simply isn't period!' he whined. Poor Tony had gone the wrong way out of Pilsner, not seen the road closed signs and suddenly was making it big in the movies! 'I don't know what was most funny – our van in the middle of the set, or me in my underpants trying to explain!' laughs Steve.

Despite their record for disasters relating to their travel arrangements, Steve and Tony were asked by Dennis and Julie Bingham, also running with Padgett sponsorship, to take their caravan to the South of France for them. Both teams had been at the German GP together and the Binghams were returning to England to take part in the TT races. They then intended to go to the South of France. The Webster equipe were heading to the South of France via Chimay in Belgium. Simon Birchall was travelling with Steve, so he could drive one of the vans. The Bingham van containing Steve and Simon was following Mick Webster as he turned in to a petrol station. The car behind Steve and Simon did not react quickly enough and not only did it hit the

Bingham's caravan, it ploughed right inside it! The caravan was ruined. Steve tried to contact the Binghams in the Isle of Man, but this proved impossible. The only thing to do was to make them a homely area in the awning. When the Binghams arrived people were full of tales about the caravan. Dennis and Julie took this to be a practical joke until they actually saw the van!

Although travelling from place to place is very exhausting and nothing like the glamorous life that is often portrayed in the media, the travelling circus of the GP world does have its moments.

'One lasting memory I have of '84 is snatching a few days' holiday at a camp site in the Rhine Valley. There were five teams who had decided to stop off at this particular site near the Rhine, a popular holiday resort with the German people. They were all happily installed with their luxury tents and motorhomes, all set out with teutonic thoroughness, when their peace was shattered by five sidecar teams rolling up. We were soon off to the local hypermarket to get crates of wine and a supply of cans. Before long the barbecues were out and a good time was had by all, by us at any rate; we were perhaps a bit too rowdy for the locals!'

Webster, as ambassador for the sport, probably managed to put more people off bike racing than those he encouraged. 'There was also a beachful of people in France,' he says, 'who were shocked by our antics. The accommodation we'd been given at Chimay was a farmer's field where the cows had only been evicted the previous day. This was fine until it rained, but once the rain water mingled with the earth the natural substances came to the surface. Our groundsheet smelled horrid. We washed it in the sea, much to the horror of the sun worshippers!' Eileen and Julie Hewitt, wife and daughter of Tony, had refused to leave the caravan at Chimay, and who can blame them? If you stood on the field, you sank up to your knees in mud and excrement!'

Apart from the myth that motor racing takes place in a flashy, tinsel-edged world is another popular misconception: that people taking part in Grands Prix have unlimited budgets and go here and there by executive jet. Some do – the well financed solo riders – but not so the Webster set- up. At least nowadays the Webster team no longer have to resort to the tactics that they used to adopt in order to make their travelling budget last. Sponsorship from P&O has alleviated the need to travel in cupboards or to be covered by a dust sheet, 'although this takes away half the fun, actually' according to Mick Webster. Back in 1984, affording fares for the ferry was somewhat of a problem for the struggling Webster. The fare would consist of a flat rate for the van and so much per person. Therefore, it might make sense for the minimum number of people to be visible and pay, and other team personnel to travel as parts! Tony Hewitt once spent two hours in a cupboard in the van, crouched on an engine with a spark plug in a most uncomfortable position. 'It was really tricky,' recalls Steve, 'there were officials near the van. So, I was trying to talk out of the side of my mouth and tell Tony that we'd come back and let him out, once these officials were gone. We climbed out of the van and the officials went away. I ran back, flung open the cupboard door and said, "Come on, quick!" Tony had cramp from being in such a confined space for so long and could not move. I saw the officials returning, so I slammed the door shut again on the moaning Tony. "Sorry pal, too f***ing late!" I said, and left poor Hewitt there for another 20 minutes.' When Karen became pregnant she was excused hiding and the team booked cabins, but even then it was 'only a two-berth for four of us,' Steve recalls.

Visions of Grand Prix stars staying in luxury hotels is also a privilege confined to the chosen few. Most teams sleep in their vans, tents or motorhomes. It does help, however, if there are enough beds or at least spaces for the whole team. In Sweden, one mechanic, Ian Carhoon, couldn't find a space to kip, so he used his initiative and slept under the van. The only snag was he omitted to tell anyone he was there, and had to roll to safety, uttering Scottish oaths, as the van pulled away in the morning, nearly squashing him!

'I really envy the big teams for one thing,' sighs Webster. Was it for the hotels, or the Lear Jets?' 'No, having a PR person to get all the paperwork through Customs,' he says. 'I have a pathological fear of Customs. Officialdom terrifies me: Police; Customs; anything like that and I'm scared s***less,' confesses Steve. 'I was once asked to untie the bike at a Customs stop and my hands were shaking so much that I couldn't unknot the rope. All my nightmares came at once when we were taken apart by Customs, all because Alan Carter didn't want his undies inspected!' Luckily father Mick is confident at dealing with officialdom and often teases Steve about his phobia of people in uniform.

Getting started in 1966: 'If you could get the sponsorship, I could be World Champion!' The first machine that Mick Webster built for his sons Steve and Kevin. (*Mick Webster*)

Cones, cones and more cones. Riding the Derbyshire/Suzuki 750 at Elvington, Steve and Kevin dislodge yet another cone during the 1980 Auto 66 Club Championship race. (*Mick Webster*)

The new pairing of Webster and Hewitt aboard the short-chassis Windle/Yamaha en route to the 1982 Marlboro Clubmans Championship. (*Mick Webster*)

The controversial long-chassis Windle/Yamaha that Webster and Hewitt had to use in 1982. 'The Windle worm' was much resented by Webster because of its unpredictable handling, and it nearly ended the racers' career in a serious accident during the Isle of Man TT. (*Mick Webster*)

The typically crowded Grand Prix paddock at Donington. (*John Colley*)

The beginning of possibly the most famous accident in sidecar racing history after Webster had lost control during the 1985 Dutch GP at Assen and sent the machine sliding across the grass ...

... ejecting Hewitt backwards into the ditch ...

... with Webster and machine in hot pursuit ...

... unearthing marshals and cameramen and providing the latter with an unexpected close-up opportunity ...

... as the sidecar continued its somersault, depositing Hewitt on his back ...

... while Webster was left to 'drown' in the pit of the 'hell' which he describes. (*Mick Webster*)

Olly Duke points to the damage after having been 'Webstered' at Cadwell Park! (*Peter Wileman*)

1987 at Hockenheim and the best kind of advertisement for Steve's backers, Dennis Trollope and Paul Seward. Webster and Hewitt's extra exertion on almost the final corner gave them victory by less than a second over the determined team of Streuer and Schneiders. (*David Goldman*)

Webster and Hewitt on the top step of the podium after their thrilling contest at the 1987 German GP. This was their second win of the season in which they went on to claim their first World Championship title. (*David Goldman*)

One of the greatest pairings in sidecar history. Steve Webster and Tony Hewitt pose for Henk Keulemans' camera.

'Once,' smiles Mick, 'we got stopped by the police on the A1. I was in the car following Steve, who was driving the bus. I saw this copper talking to Steve, so I got out to see what was the matter. The policeman told me he was dealing with the driver and would I go and wait in my vehicle. I was all ready to tell him where to go, but Steve gave me his usual terror struck glance and motioned that I should leave him to it.' 'The policeman gave the vehicle a thorough checkover and explained, very leniently, that a tacho was needed for it, and that the Websters should keep used tachographs in case of a ministry check. 'I thanked him profusely,' says Steve, taking up the story, 'and he said he'd then have a word with my dad. I felt we'd got off lightly as all he'd done was to tell us to get a tachograph and hadn't done us for not having one. I didn't want my dad to compound the situation, so I dashed down and said "just agree with everything he says, I'll explain later." I saw the policeman talking to my dad, and to my relief, my dad nodding subserviently. At last the cop headed back to his car, "Goodnight Sir", he said, "Goodnight" I grovelled, and I felt relieved when my dad also wished him "Goodnight". Ah, sighs of relief I thought, but I'd spoken too soon, for as the policeman was getting into his car, a cheeky voice shouted, "There you go, Steve, when you were singing all coppers are b*****ds, I said they weren't all bad!" With a family like that who needs enemies?'

However, this episode didn't dissuade Steve from pushing Mick into the forefront of the action. In Czechoslovakia the police came up to Steve whilst he was parked in a lay-by having his breakfast and said, 'Fahrer! Fahrer.' 'That's my dad over there,' chirped Webster, so the police promptly fined Mick for being parked in an illegal place. As Fahrer means driver, it was really Steve who should have been fined, but Mick has a broad back!

Although a lot of the way to the top of motorcycle racing is difficult and turbulent, there are many opportunities to have fun. One such occasion is the annual road race at Swananstaat, in Austria. This is a road race, but the circuit is actually far too dangerous for racing, so the riders turn up, and toddle round and collect their start money. As there is no great Championship point race going on at Swananstaat, it is an opportunity for the riders to let their hair down a bit. The first time Steve entered this race, he arrived several days early, and so, with time to kill, he and a few other riders headed to the nearest town. The town seemed to have one decent bar, so the multinational gathering of suppers and eaters strolled in to this establishment. 'It was really weird,' says Steve. 'We ordered our food and drink and kept shouting at the waiter so we could pay. Each time he replenished our drinks and walked away. There were loads of us; the Egloffs, Derek Bayley, Niall Mackenzie, Donnie McCleod, just to name a few. As the evening wore on people began to head back to the circuit. No-one appeared to be paying. Gradually the place emptied and it became apparent that the people at our table would be about the last ones there. "Oh no!" I thought, "we're were going to cop for the whole bill, which must be hundreds of pounds", so we made a dash for it. Outside were some mopeds, so six of us boarded one of them. I shared the seat with both Egloffs while my dad balanced himself on the forks like the figurehead on a ship.

We arrived at the circuit and quickly dispersed. I dived into my overalls and for some reason put a hat on to disguise myself. Seconds later a car screeched into the paddock. I busied myself with some cranks but the man came straight up to me: "You were there!" he screamed, "The bill, the bill!" "No, no!" I protested, "I've been working on this bike all night." But it was no good. He knew I'd been there and I'm not a very convincing liar. So before he fetched the police, I went around the paddock and collected the £200 we owed him. He then decided we were all big buddies and we must go back another night, which we did. While we were in there, we were approached by a local who told us he had a brother who was the Austrian equivalent of Peter Stringfellow, and would we like to go to his place? He'd even take us there in a van. Mention nightclub to racing lads and you have no trouble filling a van. Soon there were 20 of us ready to go. Simon Birchall insisted that he sat with the driver and the rest of us were crammed in the back like cattle. Soon we arrived at this big, old country house. "This looks promising", we all thought. Well, we got inside and there were only three people in there: our friend, his brother and a barman. "Oh, well, it'll liven up soon", we said. It had a least got a pin-ball machine, so we started a knock-out contest on that. We could see there was a record deck and a balcony for the DJ, so maybe it'd all get going in a minute or two. We were so engrossed in the pin-ball that we hadn't noticed Simon Birchall disappear.

When he reappeared he was absolutely stark naked; his shoes in his hand and his trousers folded like a waiter over his arm! This was the signal for the evening to degenerate. Sheppy, a mechanic, decided he'd be DJ and the disco was underway. Not a woman in the place – just 20 lads and three horrified staff. We were soon asked to leave and told we were not getting a lift back. We made it plain that there were 20 of us and only three of them, so they'd better be friendly. They *did* give us a lift back, but it was a very rough ride. We started off annoyed, but by the end of the ride the van had been on two wheels more than once. We were all so hysterical that we just piled out at the circuit and giggled our way to our vans! It isn't motor racing which is dangerous, it's the socializing that goes with it! There's nothing worse than the sidecar lads on the rampage!' exclaims Webster.

Meanwhile, back at Rowntree Mackintosh, a watchful eye was being kept on the number of days off that a certain S. Webster was taking. Steve had been lucky in making friends with a foreman who would sign his leave of absence slips and therefore by-passing the need to consult senior management. It is the policy at Rowntrees to offer a fair amount of overtime. Most workers are pleased about this as it gives them an opportunity to save for little extras. However, Steve dreaded being offered Saturday working because it really interfered with the racing. Some people could not understand his ambivalent attitude to overtime. One foreman remarked, 'I've just told that Steve Webster that if he's late again on a Saturday, there will be no more Saturdays for him!' Another worker inquired, 'Well, what's wrong with that?' 'Oh, it's not that,' continued the foreman, 'it was his reaction. When I told Webster that there would be no more Saturdays, he smiled. Most odd!'

Around this time some Rowntree workers were being offered redundancy, so the activities of all staff were carefully monitored. 'I'd got wind of the fact that I was to be called upstairs,' says Steve. 'I was asked why I needed so much time off and I explained that I was representing the country at sidecar racing. The manager then shook me by the hand and said, "You carry on, lad, stick that Union Jack where it belongs, at the front of the race!" I couldn't believe it. You could almost hear the strains of *Land of Hope and Glory*,' smiles Webster.

Steve really knew he should leave Rowntrees and pursue the world crown full-time, but by now he had met the future Mrs Webster No. 2, a girl called Karen, who was a fellow Rowntrees employee, and he felt he must provide an income. The situation sorted itself out soon enough as in the next round of redundancies Steve was asked to leave, so another era comes to an end.

Life seemed very worrying and frustrating in 1984. Steve, now supported by Karen, continued to find that the Padgett engine fell a long way short of his hopes for it. When Padgetts had said that they would supply two race-specification engines, Steve had hoped one would be a TZ500, but the better of the engines was, in fact, a Padgett development engine. Padgetts were trying to produce a Krauser-type engine, but it didn't work. 'Oh, that engine,' says Steve as he frowns, 'we nicknamed it The Padgett Brick. It was so big and heavy and we were blown off everywhere. Clive Padgett is a brilliant engineer, but the ideas he had formulated seemed to me to be about three years behind the times and as it took a year to produce the engine, it was then four years adrift. We were a laughing stock.'

Life had become a struggle. Webster had very little cash and was struggling to run. Steve was contracted to Padgetts for two years. 'One day,' he recalls, I went up to my dad's garage and my heart was in my boots. "Dad, I've made a big mistake", I moaned. Dad had found the Padgett ethic hard to accept, too. We were used to running as a family team; we just didn't realize that sponsors are not fairy godmothers. We were allowed to use Padgett vans, but sometimes they needed repairs. We would pay for these and make the van roadworthy, only to find that in the next race we'd got a different van with a new set of ailments.'

The final straw for Webster was an ill-fated trip to the French GP when the engine seized after the second practice. 'I was just packing up to go home as we had no spare engine when a fellow competitor, Derek Bayley, came to console me,' recounts Webster. Derek felt sorry for Steve and knew he had potential, so he offered Steve the loan of his practice engine. Steve used the engine and stormed home to third place, his best finish. 'I couldn't thank Derek enough,' Steve relates emotionally. I paid Derek for the wear and tear and headed home with my box of Padgett bits. Derek has since suffered a racing accident that has caused severe brain damage, and although Steve still visits him, he is always very upset to see a fine racer so reduced.

Meanwhile, in the Isle of Man, news had reached the Padgett team that young Webster had taken third at Magny Cours. They thought their engine had at last done them proud. 'When I told them I used Derek's engine and, worse still, paid him out of the prize money, I was not flavour of the month,' smiles Steve.

This was not the only time that the homecoming of our hero wiped the smiles from the faces of the Padgett family. On another occasion Webster had requested new cylinders and Dennis Bingham, who was also supported by Padgetts at that time, delivered a box of cylinders to Steve. They were two years old, but they were all that the team had available. 'We were intrigued when later that day another box arrived, to be collected by a customer of Padgetts. I shook the box and detected the unmistakable sound of cylinders rattling about. "Open it!" urged my dad, and low and behold, there they were, brand new, unavailable cylinders. My dad had suddenly grown horns. "Put 'em on, Steve. They'll be faster than these buggers!" Mission accomplished, but we were destined not to prosper as they were the wrong cylinders for our bike and we promptly seized it!' Steve was gradually collecting a box of broken engine parts. 'I decided I must say how I felt, so I went along to Peter Padgett's house and I thought, "Right, I'll get sacked, then I won't have to go on another year like this".'

Steve was met at the Padgett home by Peter Padgett, Clive Padgett, Gary Padgett, Peter's brother, and brother Alan. 'I ended up feeling like a kid in the head teacher's room,' confesses Webster. 'They wanted to know why I treated the bike as if I was a savage. I retaliated arguing that they weren't fit to sponsor people. The outcome of this exchange of views was that the Padgetts helped Steve more and more. Sacking him was the last thing on their mind. 'I was beginning to get a reputation as an upstart,' says Steve.

Despite the increased input from the Padgetts, Steve still felt they were not the right people to be with, to achieve what he wanted to achieve. The engines were still the weak link in the whole operation. A certain person had provided Steve with another race engine, but stipulated that should it be used, the Padgett name on the fairing was to be crossed out with a thin line of racer tape. 'I think the person who had so kindly helped me saw this as a bit of devilment,' smiles Steve. 'I didn't dare to do this, so I bought myself a couple of engines, and that's when I upset someone else! I decided that if I had my own engines, I could use them when I wanted and I needn't alter the sponsorship on the fairing. A good racer called Mick Barton was giving up racing and he had two cracking engines. I arranged to buy them but they were away being rebuilt. They were in the hands of a very good engine builder called Roger Keen. I had a round coming up at Donington and I rang Roger and asked him to have the engines ready for then. This gave him two weeks to have them organized. Whereas I know you can't rush a genius, as Roger would endorse, when it got to Friday night in the paddock at Donington and I had no engine at all, I was beginning to feel a bit concerned. Padgetts had promised an engine and, true to their word, turned up on Friday night, albeit at 11 o'clock, with said beast. We worked until four in the morning, installed the engine and grabbed four hours of sleep. The next day Roger triumphantly homed into view with his engine, being very sorry it was late, but parts of it had been guesting in other races! "I don't want it," I chirped, "I'm buying someone else's". Roger's face fell; he was less than happy to say the least. He put his face close to me and said, "If I see you again, Steve Webster, I may speak to you and then again I may not!" It could have been worse I guess!'

The Webster scenario was bleak, but Karen was 100 per cent behind all Steve's aspirations and attempts. Her colleagues at Rowntrees thought she must be soft, working to support a man who raced. Hard-earned money going on tyres and diesel! 'I didn't care,' says Karen, 'I believed Steve could win the World Championship and I was right behind him!' Life was hard, though. Webster couldn't keep up with the Grand Prix front runners and felt the only thing to do was give up racing. 'I think I'm growing up' he said to his father.

By the end of 1984, Steve had fallen out with almost everyone. The benevolent Dennis Trollope had relented halfway through the year and offered to help Steve out, but Steve was tied to his Padgett contract. The months ahead looked gloomy. 'The more I thought about it, I couldn't go on. If this was the way racing was, I wanted no further part in it. Paul thought I was mad, but I had had enough,' resumes Steve.

Therefore, at the end of 1984 Webster prepared to sign on the dole. As ever, father Mick was again to be the voice of reason. 'You know Paul Seward will want that chassis back, don't you?' he reminded his disconsolate son. 'He can have it,' Webster replied flatly. 'Ah well,' reasoned Mick, 'let's not be hasty. Hide the bike in cardboard boxes and let's say it's gone away to be rebuilt. It'll give us a breathing space.' Although by this stage Webster didn't care, the plan was put in action and when Mick Seward, son of Paul, arrived for the chassis, he understood why it wasn't ready. However, Mick Webster's plan didn't work completely. He intended for Steve to have a time to reflect and clear his mind, but before Steve had chance to do this a rather alarming letter arrived.

Naturally, because Steve had broken his contract with Padgetts there were loose ends to be tied up. This particular loose end took the form of a bill for £34,000 from Padgetts for parts, wear and tear, and services rendered; and a bill of this size terrified him. 'I was beginning to wonder if all that tunnelling would stand me in good stead after all,' sighs Webster. 'I can smile about it now, but I was terrified. Every time the doorbell went, I peered from behind the curtains in case it was a collection agency. I felt sick, couldn't eat, lost weight, couldn't sleep and was really ratty. I was bad tempered with my family, taking it out on all those who had made sacrifices for me, especially poor Karen. In the end Karen, level-headed and not a pathological worrier like me, suggested that I see a solicitor. I managed to turn that into a wittle. Solicitors are expensive, I had no job. Karen found out about legal aid, and so, stomach churning, I turned up at the solicitor's office seeking advice from an understanding and skilled solicitor who specialized in motorsport matters, Michael Ashley Brown. He examined the facts and told me not to worry. I was to get on with my racing; the Padgetts could not claim against me as they had not fulfilled their half of the contract either.' So, feeling relieved and renewed, Webster raced over to Flawith, unpacked the chassis and prepared to re-enter the fray!

By the time Steve had reorganized the race team, the 1984 season was effectively over. So all his energies were directed at getting the outfit up and running, to tackle the 1985 season with renewed vigour. 'Just as '84 was a year to forget, 1985 was a superb year; everything went well and winning seemed easy,' recalls Steve. During the winter of 1984 Steve had patched up his differences with Paul Seward; Paul initially having felt that Steve had been rather hot headed over the Padgett deal. But Steve had explained his case to Paul and in the end Paul agreed that he would continue to help him. Paul could see both sides of the problem and had to agree that it wasn't all Webster's fault. The deal with Paul for 1985 was that Steve could carry on using the bike and he would use his own engines. Steve had bought two engines, one from Tony Smith and another from Dennis Holmes.

'My father and I discussed our plan of attack,' says Steve, 'and it was clear that to do well, further backing was needed. We decided to paint the bike in Sikolene colours and see if we could attract a bit of backing from them. After all, this tactic had worked well in Paul Seward's case, even though we hadn't realized the significance of our colour scheme at the time. Silkolene had always been very good to us; Dennis had received help from them and some of it had benefited us, but this had been Dennis' deal whereas this venture was our own, and was by way of a bit of a "thank you". We didn't have anything else to put on the fairing anyway. Silkolene responded by giving us some help, through discounts at first and then by actual sponsorship. This was to be the start of a longstanding, productive relationship. Silkolene are great people to deal with and we have a lot of respect for each other.'

Even from early club racing days Steve had been conscious of the need to have a thorough and relevant test programme, and although finance was limited, he devised a schedule which suited him well. 'Of course,' comments Steve, 'with more finance we could have tested more components, but no matter how large your budget is there's always room for improvement. We were happy that we could decide what test we wanted and if a choice was wrong, the book stopped with us. That is the plus side of it. On the other hand, due to our inexperience, we often threw parts away that were perfect because we'd misdiagnosed a fault.'

One of the areas where the team lacked knowledge was in the engine tuning and rebuilding department. 'We'd never been brilliant with engines,' admits Steve, 'even in our club racing days. Once we went to Croft to race on the Saturday and we were due to race at Cadwell on the Sunday. It was probably one of those legendary Easter meetings which the organizers plan when they've had too much Christmas spirit. As racing enthusiasts will know, it is quite usual over the Easter weekend to find yourself at Knockhill one day and Thruxton the next. Anyway, we had gone up to Croft and seized our Suzuki triple engine. It was 2 o'clock on Saturday afternoon, so we knew that if we legged it back to Flawith we could rebuild the unit and make Cadwell the next day. We had never had to replace anything on the engine before and all we had available was a standard cylinder that didn't fit. We cut a bridge out from the inlet port using a glassfibre cutter and hacked away at parts of the engine! By midnight Saturday we had the beast rebuilt, so we tried it, but it wouldn't turn over. We'd cut so much out of it that we'd wrecked the barrel. This was Kevin's finest hour! Kev is a joiner by trade and would freely admit that he knows nothing about engines – not that he was on his own at this juncture! Then Kev, in a flash of brilliance, suggested that we left the piston ring off and then the piston wouldn't keep popping out. After all, as he correctly observed, there were a lot of fast Yams. about at the time that only had one piston ring! We tried this, and by two in the morning we had the unit turning over. The next day at Cadwell it performed marvellously and people were commenting on its power. Trial and error one, engineering expertise nil!'

During 1985, Steve spent a lot of time learning about engines from a kart engine specialist from Doncaster called Brad. 'Brad really helped tremendously,' says Steve, 'he showed me the value of being exact. He knew just how to get the best out of components and wasn't afraid to share his knowledge. He really helped me on my way. He pointed out that if you were accurate you got the best out of the power band. I might have had one exhaust port six thousandths higher than the next one and this would cause that port to come in 500 revs later, therefore shortening the power band. One cylinder would be dragging the others back. This was losing power and giving an advantage to other competitors. So, "Thank you, Brad". He taught me that engine tuning has more to it than hacking about with a big file!'

The early months of 1985 saw Brad spending a few days up at Flawith advising Steve. 'I began to realize just how much effort it takes to maintain an engine and to get it running well. I hadn't fully appreciated this before,' states Webster. This also made Steve aware of just how hard Dennis Trollope had worked on his behalf. Dennis had tried to work 36 hours a day, to give his best to his riders. Steve now knows that it is a full-time job to keep one rider supplied with competitive equipment, and even that often entails burning more than a drop of midnight oil. Dennis was trying at one point to care for Steve, Graham Wood, Keith Cousins and Steve Williams. 'Dennis would often arrive at six in the morning with a freshly rebuilt unit in the van, and say, "This'll be a flyer, lad", and I could tell that he hadn't been to bed,' says Steve. 'All-night engine building was a way of life to Dennis.'

In the back of his mind, Steve was still worried that there might be repercussions from Padgetts. People told him that the Padgetts may stop Steve from racing abroad, and on the first foreign race Steve was expecting to be impounded at the port! However, the Padgett team had no such ideas. They hoped their runners would beat Steve fair and square in the racing, but they let Steve follow his own path.

'I can see why riders have managers,' reflects Steve. 'My dad was the steadying influence throughout this period of worry. He said he would carry the can if there were any problems, but there never were. I felt a bit of an outcast, especially at Cadwell when all my ex-team mates were out to beat me. I was young and inexperienced then; I'd like to think that nowdays I could handle things better.'

Despite Steve's occasional moments of insecurity, the atmosphere surrounding the Webster team in 1985 was one of optimism, enthusiasm and hunger. Tony Hewitt was proving to be a valuable asset to the team. Not only had he calmed the hot-headed Webster down a little and developed in him a smooth and consistent riding style, he had also become very interested in the carburation aspect of the engine.

Tony is a civil engineer by trade and has a logical and analytical way of thinking. He had been talking to the Aprilia team and had become fascinated by their research into the effects of air density and humidity on the engine. Tony worked out a graph based on air density and an accompanying scale to adjust the carburation. He would be a strange sight in the Grand Prix paddock, fleeing about with his barometer, but the Webster team had the last laugh, because despite Tony looking like a deranged weather-man at times, when the other teams were trying this, that and the other setting on their jets, the Webster outfit was set up and always spot on!

'In 1985 we were really together as a team,' recalls Steve. 'Tony had got that engine kicking out 100 per cent all the time, making it easier for me to go for an intermediate gearbox. Dennis Trollope was intrigued by Tony's formula and asked for a copy. He did get a copy but a cryptic one, including a seizure-giving variable called DT! Luckily, DT (Dennis Trollope) has a good sense of humour!'

Nowdays, the Webster carburation is worked out by a computer and the readings are shared with Dennis in order to enhance friend Barry Brindley's performances. 'Well, you do share with the Brindleys,' smiles Steve, 'have you ever seen how many of them there are?! Joking apart, Barry is a good friend and he can always find vital component supplies even when parts are scarce.'

The 1985 season got off to a good start. Our pair travelled to a National round at Cadwell and clinched a win and fastest lap. This was followed by a win a month later in a National round at Brands Hatch, another lap record and then, later in April, two wins at International level. At Mallory on April 21, the pair smashed the outright circuit record. 1985 had certainly got off to a cracking start and Webster and Hewitt were very excited about their forthcoming journey to Hockenheim to take part in the German Grand Prix. 'We really should have won this one,' reflects Webster, now that he has a few more years' experience under his belt. 'It was a wet day, but it had stopped raining in time for the race. We had chosen a hard wet tyre. There are hard wets and soft wets and we had decided that a hard wet would give us most grip. Many runners had chosen the soft wet. Werner Schwarzel, who eventually claimed the victory, was on the softer compound. As the race progressed, a dry line emerged and I ploughed along on it. Now I know that I should have run for some of the time on the water, to let my tyres cool, but I hadn't the experience then. I got on the dry line and I stuck to it. I should have nursed my tyres, but I was happy to come in second. We won £3,000. This was more than an engine cost in 1985. "Crikey", we thought, "this is easy. Look how much you can win especially if you are not contracted to give half of it away!" We really were on top of the world!'

The team began to get more discerning in their engine building; the cylinders were machined by an Austrian called Hans Hummel. What with these, Tony's graph and the 110 per cent team commitment, the Webster team were really confident. 'We felt we could do it. It was all coming together. Indeed, we were ready to take on the world!' After this success Steve and Tony went on to achieve a third place, on the podium again, in Salzburg. This represented more cash in the racing pot and things really seemed to be looking up! To put the icing on the cake, the pair won the British Championship at Donington and set a new 500cc lap record.

Things were going just too well. Then came ASSEN. Even people who have never heard of Webster and Hewitt have seen the now famous clip of the duo speeding into the ditch at Assen in 1985. Having already notched up an impressive chain of results, Steve and Tony were hungry to win. As Steve sped past the pits at the Dutch circuit, Mick held out a pit board that declared that they had a six second lead. '"Six seconds", I remember thinking,' says Steve, '"that's not much".' Clear in his mind that six seconds was no sort of lead at all, Steve went on to break the lap record. All this was achieved in damp conditions, which are the very hardest to race in as they tend to make the track very greasy. 'This is when my lack of experience caught me out,' confesses Steve. 'I could feel the outfit going into a slide, but I still thought it would be all right. I knew I was going on to the grass, but I figured if I sat up a bit, I could control the bike. I sat up; we went sideways, then backwards, and then that moment when all you think is "bloody hell" and you wait for the impact! It came, a bang – and then I was aware of my helmet filling up with water. I was convinced that I was drowning, but in fact I wasn't underwater at all. I had been, but now I was out; I tried and tried to push my visor up but my arm wouldn't work. I very quickly deduced that my left arm was broken and I had enough sense to push up my visor with my right. I then remembered Clive Padgett, and the fact that he had had an accident and broken his arms and the marshals not being aware of this had assisted him by pulling his arms; the result being he still had problems with one of his arms. I quickly lay on the ground, on my busted arm, and motioned to the marshals that it was broken. They realized what I meant and went for a stretcher. I was also looking for Tony at this time. Hewitt was being loaded on to a stretcher. In fact, in true Laurel and Hardy fashion, we arrived at the ambulance on our separate stretchers at the same moment. To say, "Another fine mess you've got me into", would have been quite fitting for Tony at that moment! We compared notes: "You all right?" "Yeah! You all right? Me arm's bust." "Yeah, my back's killing me!" It went on in this way as we lay side-by-side on our journey to hospital!'

Steve ended up with a plate in his arm and Tony was told there was no permanent damage, although years later it was discovered that he had in fact crushed two vertebrae in this accident. The worst bit was probably yet to come, the post mortem on how it happened.

'I blamed everything,' smiles Steve, 'the tyres, yes, they must have gone off at a critical moment; the bike, could have been a handling problem. In car racing circles there's a saying amongst long-suffering mechanics that the biggest problem on a racing car is the nut behind the wheel. Well, I don't know what the sidecar equivalent is, but I'm it. There was one cause of that accident at Assen, the Webster! When I saw videos of the crash, I couldn't believe it. There I was, flat-out through the complex, into the left hand corner. I should have gone down two gears, but no, Webbo powers on, flat in sixth; it was bound to end in tears!' For a long time after, Webster treated this area of the Assen circuit with a lot of respect. He almost developed a mental block about that particular corner. 'We went back to Assen later in '85 and Tony remarked that he might as well get off at that point as I was so slow. It is true; other outfits were nearly running into the back of us. I don't think I'm still completely over the ghost of that little dip,' Steve admits.

Just as this corner at Assen preys on Steve's mind, an experience that he had whilst acting as rider's representative has coloured his judgment about an area of the Salzburg circuit. 'Like the early episode with the cones at Elvington, you see one thing when you are standing up and another when you are on a bike. Walking around the circuit at Salzburg, I saw an area where if you went off you'd hit Armco with spikes in it. Admittedly, you'd have to launch your outfit to do it, but it is possible and so, being the calm, composed, cool person that I am,' laughs Steve, 'I worry about that now.'

On a serious note, he does find it hard to wipe from his mind corners or parts of circuits where friends have succumbed to fatal or serious accidents. 'I try not to think about it,' says Steve 'but there are certain places that you can't pass without remembering a friend or colleague lost in the name of sport.'

Assen left both Steve and the bike in a mess. Mick, level-headed and organized as ever, suggested that they go straight from Assen to Switzerland to get the bike repaired at Louis Christian's place. Meanwhile, Steve had no alternative but to lie and sunbathe, whilst his arm healed. Steve's arm was not totally better for the next Grand Prix at Silverstone, but on the advice of his family doctor Steve decided to go ahead and race. As it happened, all he did was practice as bad weather caused the meeting to be stopped. It appears even the gods were on Steve's side!

The next outing was back to Assen; the Webster in tentative mood, collecting a first in practice, but failing to finish in the race.

1985 finished happily; Webster's first GP win had eluded him but the season still left him with a warm glow inside telling him that he had made the right decision, upon which to capitalize in 1986.

But the new season got off to a disappointing start; Steve and Tony failing to finish at the Nurburgring due to a seized engine. They sat and watched Biland being tormented by Streuer, who went on to win the race, leaving Rolf literally jumping up and down in the cockpit. In Austria they powered into a second place finish and managed the same in Assen. It was in the fourth round of the World Championship that they clinched the winner's laurels. At Spa, in the appalling wet conditions, they ran on the limit and crossed the line in fearless glory. Steve recollects that conditions were awful because there was running water on the track and that they were on the limit all the way through the race. 'How we didn't crash, I just don't know. We locked up on the corners and I was still a bit wild in those days. At Eau Rouge we aquaplaned, but used the gravel to regain some grip. There we were at 130mph-plus, flying up the hill and bottoming out at Eau Rouge. There were rivers of water all over the place and we bounced in and out of them in a red haze. Egbert was out early on and the victory was ours. That's a race I'll never forget. I wouldn't win in those conditions today; I've lost the "mad dog" mentality and become aware that I am flesh and bone, but then winning was all that was on my mind. It was a wonderful moment when that chequered flag dropped.'

1986 brought increased sponsorship; Silkolene and Paul Seward were still supporting the team, but now Avon Tyres also entered the equation. '1986 was the first year that we enjoyed Avon's sponsorship,' says Steve. 'We had used their tyres for a while and at first they gave us a discount and then firmer sponsorship. Rolf Biland had used Avon tyres for many years, but later swapped to Yokohama. I know there are those who dub me "Mr Standard" because I do tend to go for consistency and not try a lot of new products, but my relationship with Avon has prospered as time has gone on and I feel a lot of beneficial development work has come out of a long-term relationship.'

A deal for the 1986 season was also put to Steve by Masato Kumano, a well known Japanese sidecar racer. Masato had decided that he wished to retire from racing and that he would like to run his own team. He put together a package for Steve which was absolutely marvellous. Steve would be paid to ride and Masato would provide everything including a pot of very prestigious computer sponsorship. Steve was overjoyed; then one clause followed another, and Steve would have to live in Germany. Perhaps he wouldn't get a wage; maybe he would need to provide certain items, and gradually this ace deal disintegrated into a poor deal, and Steve was searching for extra backing again.

At this point Steve renewed his relationship with Dennis Trollope. It had become apparent to Steve when he had split with Dennis and courted the Padgetts, that Dennis was indeed an angel of a man, and Steve was more than happy to be able to renew his relationship with him. Dennis was to supply engines, transport and parts, and in return Webster was to pay a percentage of his prize money. The transport took the form of the Fowlers of Bristol bus and the engines were good Yamahas; Dennis has strong ties with Yamaha, and he was just as serious about winning the World Championship as Webster and Hewitt were. The Dennis and Steve partnership was on a firmer footing than ever before. Mr Trollope knew Steve had journeyed along the learning curve and was capable of winning, and Steve was allowed much more of a free hand than in earlier times. However, although Dennis tried to help all he could, his efforts only showed them how, unconsciously, they had established their own set routine as a team; and when Mick went on holiday and Dennis helped them in Sweden, the routine fell apart. 'We finished 15th and we blamed poor Dennis,' it probably wasn't his fault, but we were so in tune as a team and couldn't do things in a different order. Dennis' routine was just as effective, but it upset our rhythm. It's a good job he realized the gearbox problems were coincidence and doesn't take offence!'

Sweden and finishing 15th was a blot on an otherwise consistent season, but as ever something was stirring in Webster's mind and he was thinking to himself that, 'what I really need now is a Krauser engine. Is there a way I can get one?'

7

The Championship Years

Unlike the episode of the LCR chassis, which caused him to go his own separate way from Dennis Trollope, the acquisition of the Krauser engine was to be a project that they would work on together. Mick Webster also played a major part in the negotiations with Krauser. 'We started off like a clip from "Fawlty Towers"' laughs Steve: 'My dad is famous for his straight talking and I could forsee some sticky moments in Germany. "Don't mention the war", I urged him, so what did he do? First topic: the war, but as an ex-aircraft engineer, the conversation was one of praise for the design and reliability of German tanks and bombers.' Mike Krauser Senior and Mick got on like a house on fire. The Germans are sticklers for etiquette and Mike Krauser appreciated Mick's family involvement with the team and liked his genuine approach. After a short conversation, he was more than willing to be associated with the team. Mike Krauser had also tried his hand at grasstrack racing, so he and Mick had a lot in common. The Websters were the first British team that Mike Krauser had helped.

The engine that the Webster equipe were using until 1987 was based on the old inline four-cylinder Yamaha design. It had conventional piston port induction and had last been used by the works solo teams in 1980. The Krauser design was still an inline configuration as opposed to the newer V4 designs of the works teams in the 500cc solo class, but had the benefit of reed-valve crankcase induction. This new design allowed the sidecar racers to use much more modern cylinders and produced significantly more power over a wider rev range, whilst still allowing them to use the Yamaha crankshafts. A Krauser engine was also purchased by

Derek Bayley, and Derek and Steve worked together – not always with Dennis' knowledge – to act as their own little development team. This proved to be a very valuable liaison. Derek and Steve were the only riders in Britain running Krausers. They pooled their testing information and this was extremely beneficial. Rolf Biland had used a Krauser, but was anxious to keep any 'tweeks' he'd discovered close to his chest. 'Together Derek and I found out all kinds of things,' remarks Webster; 'for example, the oil pump casting was machined for a bearing housing and the oil pump kept falling off. We also discovered that some bearings were machined too deep and the bearing cases got hot and everything moved around. Derek and I unearthed all kinds of things, and by the start of the season we'd got the engines just as we wanted them.'

At the start of the racing season in March, there are lots of National fixtures and Derek and Steve used these as 'up tempo' test sessions and gradually the Krauser got better and better. The feedback between our two would-be race development engineers was tremendous.

'Of course I can't do much without causing controversy,' Steve wistfully sighs; 'we got involved in a debate about Krauser engines that led to a court case. I hasten to add we were not directly involved, but it taught us that you sometimes can't even pass comment on things without it being blown out of all proportion. To try to put the record straight, any engine when you first get it requires some development. What I might like out of an engine's performance would not be suitable for another rider. We all have our own style, our personal likes and dislikes. You can't just stick engines in and away you go, not to get the best out of them, that is.

'Other people acquired Krausers at the same time as Derek and myself but they did not tackle testing the engines in the same way that we did. For us, the mutual support through testing worked well. Progin and Brookes had also tried Krauser and were unhappy. A journalist picked up on Progin's discontent and asked my dad, off the cuff, whether ours was fit to race when we got it. Dad explained how Derek and I had sorted our engines out. However, this chance conversation was used out of context and my dad was invited to go to Court in Switzerland, where Progin and Charlie Auf der Maur were having a legal battle about the performance of the Krauser, to say his piece. Needless to say he had no interest in any such projects. We won our first World Championship with a Krauser; I think that says it all.'

The man who machines all the parts for Krauser is this real character called Charlie Auf der Maur. He also produces a race unit called the ADM. The relationship between Mick and Charlie got off to a bad start due to a misunderstanding of Mick's rather lively dry wit. Charlie's English is not amazingly fluent; however, it is better than Steve's German. Charlie has picked up words in everyday use and one of his favourites is 'bullshit'. He gets very excited when describing the workings of the engine and if he detects displeasure, he will punctuate the explanation with a few sprinklings of the term. Due to his propensity for this phrase, Mick has christened him Charlie Bullshit. Unfortunately for Mr Auf der Maur, this name has stuck. At first Charlie thought this label was a slight on his workmanship, but eventually Mick has made him see the funny side of it.

'You always know it's Charlie on the telephone,' grins Steve 'when the conversation goes: "Steve, how can you say where I am at now, the measurements must I have now it", but, compared with my German that's very, very good indeed and I'm not bullshitting!'

After the early season testing, Webster and Hewitt prepared to go to the Spanish Grand Prix. Just to be on the safe side, Webster had a last minute talk with Harold Bartols, who was able to suggest a couple of fine adjustments. Off they went to Spain and to their delight the Krauser was a rocket ship, and they powered to first place with the greatest of ease. Biland's similar LCR Krauser claimed pole position, but when the lights turned to green it was the British pairing that swept into the lead. Webster and Hewitt lost the lead briefly to Biland and Waltisperg on lap seven, but soon overtook the Swiss duo, who were forced to retire with brake problems. Egbert Streuer lost his passenger, Bernie Schnieders, while Alain Michel finished 40 seconds adrift in second place. Dennis Trollope was pleased with the way that the season had started. The press described Webster and Hewitt as 'destroying the opposition in the searing heat of Jerez'. Dennis felt free to concentrate on Steve Williams and Graham Wood and let Webster steer the Dennis Trollope flagship under his own steam. Mick is a capable and well-organized team manager and engineer, and the

Flawith premises were a hive of activity. Dennis continued to build the cranks and the Webster team did the rest.

The second Grand Prix of the sidecar season was held at the high-speed Hockenheim circuit in Germany and resulted in the second victory of the year for the Yorkshiremen. This race was very different from Spain. Although Webster had clinched pole position, he could not shake off the determined Streuer, who slipstreamed past Steve on the 14th and final lap. Hockenheim consists of two long straights, broken up by chicanes, and a tight, twisty infield section surrounded by massive grandstands seating over a 100,000 people. Steve knew that if Streuer led into the stadium on the last lap, it would be virtually impossible for him to pass the Dutchman. Webster and Hewitt made a monumental effort to outbrake Streuer and Schneiders at the fast right-hand bend leading into the stadium and they succeeded – just! For the remaining part of the lap – about three quarters of a mile – the battling sidecars were mere inches apart. Streuer attempted to go round the outside of Steve on the final corner but failed by less than a second, having to accept second best on this occasion to the new British Championship contenders. There was a slight hiccup when the Austrian Grand Prix was reintroduced to the calendar and Mick Webster, seeing there was a clear weekend, had booked a holiday. The Austrian Grand Prix was reinstated at the last minute and Mick couldn't change his plans. So once again Dennis stepped in, and this time introduced the notion of carburating each cylinder differently. Poor Tony's graph was out of the window now and Webster was a worried man. The team came in fourth and were lucky to manage that. Mick is now banned from holidays unless the season is well and truly over!

Following numerous problems in practice, Steve and Tony had to wait for the final session before they could guarantee a place on the grid. They finally qualified second to Streuer, but were far from confident after all the practice dramas. However, the race turned out to be an absolute cracker. The top four sidecar crews in the world put on a dramatic show with many changes of position and quite a few accidental contacts between the battling outfits. At one point in this frantic race Steve ran into the back of Alain Michel with such force that he smashed the front of his fairing. At other times, the warring crews were three or four abreast whilst lapping at an average of nearly 108mph! Eventually Rolf Biland scored his first win for two years, with Streuer second and Michel third, after Webster had tried to overtake both his rivals on the fast right-hand bend at the bottom of the hill on the last lap. Steve and Tony were lucky to finish fourth when this rather optimistic overtaking effort failed and they spun at very high speed.

After this slight setback, the pair went on to record a second place at Assen. The race was held in appallingly wet conditions and Streuer totally dominated his home Grand Prix, leaving Webster and Hewitt to drive conservatively in the dangerous conditions to finish 24 seconds adrift.

If the competitors thought that Assen was wet, they had to readjust their views for the French Grand Prix at Le Mans. The rain was so heavy that it was impossible to see the outfit in front until you actually ran into it! Webster qualified in second place, nearly a second behind Biland, who was beginning to get his Krauser engine working really well. In the race, Rolf pulled away to a secure lead and so missed a fantastic battle between the other major Championship contenders. Steve battled through to hold second place, but a spin in the treacherous conditions demoted him to third behind Alain Michel. Shortly after retaking second place Webster spun again, this time rejoining in fourth place behind Streuer. In the closing stages, Streuer overtook Michel and looked to be comfortably in second place, but he had not counted on the gritty determination of the Yorkshire pairing who had recovered from their spin and powered through almost to snatch second place on the last lap! Steve and Tony were forced to settle for third, but had the consolation of setting the fastest lap of the race in their demonic charge back to the front. Due to the horrible conditions their fastest lap was some 20 seconds outside the lap record.

On then to Donington and the British Grand Prix, described by Steve as 'real dingbat of a race'. It is hardly surprising that the spectators leapt over the barriers at the end of the 24-lap race. It had been a unforgettable three way battle, with former champions Biland and Waltisperg and current champions Egbert Streuer and Bernard Schnieders. The lead was constantly changing. Five laps from the finish Webster grabbed the lead, and the crowd went wild! Biland retired with an ignition problem, and a British victory was claimed for the first time since 1980.

However, on a cool afternoon at Anderstorp all their ambitions were going to come to fruition. Not many people have a special place in their hearts for Anderstorp. It is a very expensive place to get to and the 2.5-mile circuit is rather run down, but to Webster and Hewitt, it is remembered as paradise. However, it was not a victory that was won without controversy, but in the end everyone was smiling on the podium.

'I recall the race very clearly,' says Webster; 'for 19 laps, Biland and I were swapping the lead, with Egbert and Bernie in a comfortable third. We constantly outbraked each other at the end of the main straight. The right-hand Atlas curve at the end of the main straight looked like a possible passing place. Four laps from the end Streuer retired and the Championship was ours, but you always want to win, or at least in those days I did. I probably had learned by Le Mans in 1991 to arrive in a comfortable third and definitely win!

'So, I battled on with Biland to try to gain the lead. On the last lap, I closed on to Biland's tail as we braked into the Atlas curve. Coming out of Atlas, Biland drifted a little wide and I pulled alongside. Biland pulled across and our outfits collided. I lost my wheelarch and mudguard and I limped across the line, but the World Championship was ours,' Steve reflects.

This had been achieved by a combination of talent and dogged determination. The support that our duo received from Mick Webster and Dennis Trollope was invaluable. Mick had ensured reliability and consistency and Dennis had employed the tactics that had helped Jock Taylor to triumph seven years earlier. How proud Jock would have been! Therefore the target now was 1988 and retaining the World crown.

'You could entitle this bit, "Webbo goes off again",' laughs Steve. 'For 1988, I knew that I wanted two Krauser engines; a spare race-spec engine is vital. It is possible to run with one engine, but with two you have that insurance that if there is a problem you can still run. It is ideal to have a good rest before race day because if you are up all night building up your one and only unit, not only are you exhausted, you are also very stressed-up, and that is the worst enemy of a racer.'

'I had realized after Sweden and Czechoslovakia, where a wrong tyre choice led to coming home in third, that the other lads who had new engines had a power advantage. I couldn't run in 1988 with a year-old engine because to challenge for the World Championship effectively, you need tip-top equipment. Dennis couldn't afford two new engines, so I decided I had better try to make a deal under my own steam. I approached Krauser direct and they were more than happy to help. I got two free engine cases as a reward for winning. If I had known that I could get the cases, Dennis and I might have been able to work something out. Anyway there was no animosity on either side about me "going off" again, but it would have been good to keep the link with Dennis. We are still very good friends and I continue to get my parts from Fowlers of Bristol.'

In 1988, Steve and Tony had backing from Silkolene and Avon, when a new and very exciting sponsor was about to enter the frame. 'Paul Seward has always kept an ear to the ground hunting for sponsors on our behalf,' says Steve. 'I knew that Paul couldn't commit himself to a chassis, but he did say he'd been talking to other sponsors for us. To be frank, I thought that Paul was just trying to let us down gently, I didn't really think that there were any other sponsors in the offing. However, he had been talking to Brown Brothers, a firm who sold heavy plant to the construction industry. He had said that they expressed an interest, but this often happens and then comes to nothing, so I hadn't particularly thought about Browns until one day when I got a rather intriguing phone call. It went: "Now then, what will it cost to jump into bed with you?" – not the sort of request I get on a daily basis! This was the opening line from Ron Brown. He had talked to Paul and was very keen, basically wanting to know what it would take to become a sponsor. I explained to Ron Brown that £60,000 would just about make it perfect; Ron arranged a meeting and very quickly agreed. This was the first time I actually felt like a World Champion. To be asked what I wanted instead of having to beg and grovel was wonderful! This deal seemed perfect!'

Steve has nothing but praise for the Brown Brothers: 'They are genuinely nice people, they made every effort to treat me well and they are still firm family friends.'

Steve Webster and Gordon and Ron Brown had a great deal of mutual respect. They encouraged and inspired each other but they never expected Steve to neglect his race preparations in order to talk to race day guests. They would point out who the guests were, if Steve and Tony had time, but they never ever demanded; they seemed the ideal sponsors. They had a love of the sport and their enthusiasm was infectious. Both would visit Steve and Tony outside of race day commitments and treat the sportsmen plus their wives to nights out where the topics of conversation were broad and varied. 'They were thoroughly entertaining people,' says Webster, 'jovial hosts, who really got pleasure from others having a good time. Sometimes racing wouldn't even be mentioned. They were never pushy or overbearing and never ever gave you the feeling that they were doing you a big favour. Some sponsors can make the riders feel very inferior and uncomfortable. With some backers you are afraid to say much for fear of putting your foot in it and losing their support, but it was not like this with Gordon and Ron.'

Being a very down to earth character Steve appreciates straight talking and no flannel. 'From that point of view, Gordon Brown was spot on. You knew just where you stood with him. If I'd go down to their office to talk to them, I knew straight away, if I was welcome to talk or if I'd better make myself scarce. Gordon would say, "Ay up, lad, don't pull up a chair you're not stopping" or "What brings you here? Sit down and I'll organize the coffee."

'The Browns' filing system was a joy to behold. 'There were three drawers,' remembers Steve, 'the papers in the top drawer were things which must be paid and our bills were always in the bottom drawer. If a payment was late and I'd pop in to sort it out, Gordon would dive in the drawer and proclaim "I'm on with it lad, I'm on with it!"'

If Gordon had time he'd talk to Steve for hours, he really wanted to help the pair all he could. He was so impressed after they had won the 1988 Championship that he told Webster that he would like an option on him. Steve, thinking this sounded a bit sinister, wondered if this was an alternative to someone having a contract out on him, and thought he had better go into this in a bit more detail.

'Sounds fine, but what does it mean?' asked Webster.

'Well,' said Gordon, 'as you've done so well, we'd like first shout on you for next season. Now we may take you on or we may not, but we want first option.' 'Oh, OK.' said Steve, thinking that would be that, but no sooner had Steve agreed than Gordon was on the phone detailing his solicitor to draw up a contract of an option of intent. The solicitor had this in the office within minutes and Gordon was soon busy recruiting a witness. When the tea lady came in she was asked to witness the deal. 'Look here,' said Gordon Brown, 'I'm giving Steve Webster £1' (money has to change hands to make the option valid) 'and he is agreeing that I have an option on his services. Can you witness this?' The bemused tea lady muttered something about 'Oh, £1, very nice', and trotted off with her trolley, no doubt gaining a very curious impression about the world of sponsorship!

So, with additional sponsorship and a new member of the team – a mechanic known as Sheppey, who had worked with Martin Wimmer and Helmut Faff, the great innovator in sidecar racing – preparations for 1988 began.

By the start of 1988 there had been additions to the Webster family as well. Steve now had a baby daughter, Holly, and he felt he needed to spend more time at home. 'The idea was,' recounts Steve, 'that with Sheppey at the workshop, I would have more time with the family. In fact, I was out more. We would discuss tweeks and innovations and I didn't want to miss out on trying things. Also there were team meetings at the "local" and these tended to drag on a bit. So what I thought would free me, tied me down even more. After 1988 we realized we didn't really need extra personnel, and reverted to running as a family team.'

The concept of someone being World Champion does tend to paint a picture of a large back-up team. This is indeed true in the case of the well-financed solo riders. They are supported by a cast of what looks like thousands. It is hardly surprising therefore that a passing lorry driver, who spotted Steve in the cab of the transporter, took him to be not an elevated world class sportsman, but a truck driver.

'It was quite funny really,' chuckles Steve; 'there I was sitting in the truck, when another lorry pulled up alongside.
"You've got a cushy number haven't you?" the driver chirped.
"Me?"
"Yes, I bet you get all round the world with this lot don't you?"
"Oh, here and there."
"How many drivers have you got then?" asked the trucker.

"Just me."

"Ah well. If he needs any more will you mention me. I've got my Class 1 HGV", the fellow went on.

"Oh, I shouldn't bother," I said very seriously; "he's a real b****rd to work for!"

"I thought so, I've seen him on telly! See ya pal!", replied the driver and went on his merry way!'

1988 saw another change; a slight feeling that Steve and Tony were not as close as they had been in the beginning. Winning the World Championship had been a marvellous reward for all the team and they each reacted to it in their own way. Steve understates his talent, he doesn't push himself forward, and becoming World Champion didn't change him at all. Tony, rightly, felt that being World Champion should bring some accolades, and this led to one or two differences of opinion.

'I remember when we were at a charity event in Harrogate, in aid of the St John's Ambulance Brigade. At the last minute they told us that they wanted us in our leathers, and we had to run across the street and get changed in the truck. I remarked to Tony that I felt ridiculous walking through Harrogate in my leathers on a Saturday night,' recalls Steve. "Don't be silly," came Tony's sharp reply, "walk like a World Champion and be proud." I didn't feel like this though, I was delighted to be World Champion, but I still don't feel I can act like a celebrity. I really envy Frank Bruno. He can say how good he is, and make it all sound acceptable. I'd hate to come across as big-headed or self-opinionated, because I'm not. Striking the balance is very hard. I suppose it's back to the haves and the have nots. A solo World Champion would have a Porsche and a Lear Jet. Kurt Waltisperg has a Porsche and this always rankled Tony. Kurt can afford a Porsche because of his business interests, not due to his racing endeavours, I'm sorry to say. Tony was the second most highly paid passenger, but his earnings fell a long way short of Porsche category. That's sidecars I'm afraid!'

Therefore, 1988 began with Steve and Tony edging in slightly different directions when it came to promoting themselves, but with Mick at the helm the team was pulled together and the battle began.

The first Grand Prix of the year was on May 1, at the 2.621-mile track in Jerez, Spain. This was in fact the Portuguese Grand Prix, but the track at Estoril was not passed on safety grounds, so the event was relocated to Spain. However, the Portuguese government were less than happy about this. They did not want their name associated with the event and they hoped the adverse publicity about Estoril would be played down. In the end, the event was called the Gran Premio Expo '92, having been sold to a high bidder for advertising purposes. This was nearly as confusing as the 'Not the Brazilian Grand Prix'!

'We were very tense,' recalls Steve. 'It's always a nail-biting situation in any race, but the first round of defending your World title had an extra edge to it. It didn't help that the main topic of conversation in the paddock was the fantastic practice lap that Biland had put in. He'd clocked up a lap faster than the solo lads. Added to this bit of psychological warfare, the weather was very changeable and we weren't too sure what tyre choice to go for. We'd qualified two seconds behind Biland which was a hell of a lot to make up in greasy, drizzly conditions. Biland was actually the first casualty of the weather as he spun off on the second lap. Soon the drizzle turned to a heavy downpour. Although I was leading, I had to raise my hand to halt the race, as I couldn't see a thing.'

Once the conditions improved, a second leg was run over 19 laps. Rival Biland was back in the frame but a good 9.4 seconds down on the current World Champions. 'Looking at the sky, I'd gambled on a hard rear tyre,' confesses Steve, 'a mistake as it happened, as I slipped around all over the place and Rolf just reeled us in. Over five laps he made up the 9.4-seconds deficit and went on to win, Streuer was in second place and I was a relieved third. That was one of those races that's like banging your head against a brick wall,' says Webster 'lovely when it stops! The only consolation of the day was claiming fastest lap.'

So it was back to Flawith for more preparation and to get ready for a visit to the Nurburgring. The sidecar teams were not very pleased about racing on the Saturday as it seemed to be another occasion when they were labelled as the Cinderellas of the sport. But the races were to be televised, to be seen live on the Saturday; this at least ensured that the sidecar teams' efforts would be seen. When the sidecar class is scheduled to be shown after the 500s it very often gets cancelled if the 500 race overruns, but on this occasion the sidecar boys were also to get the benefits of the best of the weather. On the Sunday it would pour down, whereas Saturday was a perfect day. Webster and Hewitt, who had qualified second, stormed away from the line and into the lead. However, it wasn't to be held for long as Biland, who had been in pole position, soon snatched it back. The race turned into a five-way battle royal between Webster and Hewitt, Biland and Waltisperg, the Zurbrugg brothers, Alain Michel and Jean Marc Fresc and Streuer and Schneiders. Actually, Streuer was just there for the hell of it; he had been left on the line with a broken gear linkage bolt, and was three laps behind but still mixing it with the best of them. Webster's heart missed a beat when Biland's engine suddenly died, yet it turned out only to be a hiccup and although this gave Steve a chance to grab the lead, Biland soon gained it back. On lap seven the Zurbruggs took the lead, snatching it from under Rolf's and Steve's noses. Martin Zurbrugg wore his boot away during this race and ended up with a badly damaged and profusely bleeding toe. The Zurbruggs were amazingly tough; anyone else would have retired, but Martin considered this a mere flesh wound. Webster repassed and held on to the lead again until the last lap, when wily Biland powered past him, collecting the laurels and the lap record. A pattern was being set at this early stage of the season that was to continue until the last race.

The next port of call was Austria and this was a venue that Webster faced with trepidation. 'The circuit at the Salzburgring is very quick and very dangerous. By 1988, I had become the FIM's representative and one of the dubious pleasures of this role was to be invited to do safety inspections at various tracks. I had completed a safety inspection at the Salzburgring and I noticed hazards whilst walking around that you would never be aware of when crouched over the bike. This probably accounts for my poor practice qualification, fourth. In your mind you think, "if I go off here, there are spikes at the other side of that Armco". There are definitely certain situations when ignorance is bliss!'

The actual race at the Salzburgring was breathtaking, the dicing on the fast and twisty circuit showing both precision and commitment. Biland and Waltisperg made it three in a row here and Steve finished third, crossing the line at 120mph, only half a second behind Michel who was in second place. Biland had driven a faultless race and finished with a two second lead. The pressure was on for the World Champion.

'It didn't help,' remarks Steve, 'that I had been asked by Pete Hillaby to become the FIM representative for the sidecars. I was totally the wrong person for the job and the responsibilty of this role had added to my problems.' Early in 1988 Steve had been approached by Pete Hillaby, then Chairman of the ACU and a member of the FIM's CCR, the road racing governing body, to act as the rider's representative on the FIM's sporting commission. The solo riders already had a representative in Sito Pons, but the general feeling was that the sidecar competitors needed their own spokesman as their needs were not being put forward at FIM meetings. Steve had many doubts about accepting the responsibility, feeling that he had neither the experience nor the time to represent his fellow competitors adequately, but he allowed himself to be talked into accepting the position, being told that he would only need to attend one meeting per year, which was the FIM Plenary Commision conference.

Steve is quick to point out that he had no concept of the politics involved in the government of the sport. Indeed, to this day he remains relatively naive in the art of politicking and making political allies. He also admits to being a slow reader, taking time to digest important pieces of information. Thus it isn't difficult to imagine his horror when the correspondence from the FIM began to flow through his letter box. He would arrive back at home, having worked on the outfit all day and most of the night, to be confronted by the discussion notes for the next FIM meeting. Steve says that he was receiving two or three packages a week, each one being as thick as a London telephone directory. As he started to read these tomes, he felt an overwhelming sense of panic: what did he know about the technical specification of snowmobiles or the need to control the use of special fuels in drag racing?

Eventually Steve realized that he did not need to become an authority on every aspect of motorcycle sport, that he was only called to comment on the aspects of the sport in which he was directly involved. That major hurdle overcome, one would have expected Steve's political career to become much easier, but unfortunately, that proved not to be the case. Instead, his straight talking honesty was his downfall on many occasions, his lack of political dishonesty making him very unpopular with other members of the FIM committee. He tried desperately to represent his fellow sidecar competitors, always seeking to put their feelings and grievances before the FIM jury meetings, and often with very little input from the other riders. As Steve points out, it wasn't because the sidecar competitors did not care what was happening at the FIM meetings that they appeared to take so little interest, it was simply the fact that they were too busy working on their machines to find time to involve themselves in the politics and government of the sport.

Steve Webster took his new found responsibilities very seriously, to the point where his involvement in representing the riders had a detrimental effect on his own performance. He would often have to break off from preparing his own machine to attend an FIM meeting. On one occasion, during practice at the Nurburgring, he left a job unfinished to attend an FIM jury meeting and promptly seized his engine because he had forgotten to fill the radiator with water! The consequences of this oversight could have been disastrous. Fortunately the only damage was to the machine's engine. The effect of a high-speed seizure can often be a massive accident, causing the driver to lose control as the machine's rear wheel locks solid. This was not an isolated incident, for on another occasion he assembled a crankshaft incorrectly when he was interrupted by Masato Kumano's wife wanting to know why Masato had been black-flagged in the previous practice session.

Steve's involvement as the riders' representative on the FIM led to numerous arguments with his father. Mick maintained that Steve could not carry out his duties at the FIM and prepare his machine at the same time. Mick pointed out to Steve that, unlike Sito Pons, he did not have an army of mechanics to carry out the work on the bike and that he was putting his and Tony Hewitt's life at stake by having to rush his preparation in order to attend the jury meetings. Although Steve agreed with this sentiment, he felt that someone ought to represent the sidecar interests. Unlike the 500cc class, the sidecar competitors were for the most part amateurs who did not have team managers, PR staff and marketing people to represent them at the meetings, so their views and interests would not be aired if he failed to speak for them.

In an effort to improve the conditions and remuneration of his fellow sidecar competitors, Steve managed to alienate himself with a large number of them. He had been badgering Mike Trimby of IRTA for a considerable time to get a better deal for the sidecars, feeling that they were always last in the queue where money and conditions were concerned. Mike Trimby's response was to take Steve for a walk through the paddock, pointing out the scruffy vans, dirty awnings and generally unkempt appearance of the sidecar racing fraternity, comparing this with the immaculate, super professional image of the major 500 and 250 teams. Trimby said that when the sidecar teams presented a better image then, and only then, would he be interested in doing anything about their rewards. If they didn't do something about their appearance, he added, there would be no place at all for the class in future Grand Prix meetings.

The realization that Mike Trimby was serious in his threat to get rid of the sidecar class prompted Steve to take action. He drafted a letter to all the sidecar teams, having it translated into several languages, which spelled out the areas where they must improve if they wanted to be acceptable to IRTA. He even went as far as to try to set up a clothing manufacturer to supply free overalls to the poorer teams at the back of the field, so that they would look smart on the grid in front of the television cameras.

Not unnaturally, some of the smaller teams took great exception to Steve's letter, pointing to the fact that they would rather spend their meagre budgets on new tyres than having their van repainted. Some of them even refused to speak to Steve, saying that he had no right to criticize their efforts; after all, it was all right for him, he had sufficient money to present an acceptable image; they were operating on a shoestring, most of them holding down a job during the week and racing at the weekend on the money they earned. So Webster's great initiative to improve the lot of his fellow competitors merely served to drive a wedge between them, distancing the sidecar class even further from IRTA and the well-funded teams at the top of the sport.

As a four times World Champion Steve has demonstrated his cool self-control and unflappable determination on numerous occasions on the world's racetracks. Therefore it is strange that his role as rider's representative should have had such a profound effect on his nerves. He freely admits that the pressures of this responsibility prevented him from eating or even sleeping properly. So important was it for him to do a good job for his friends and rivals that he often neglected his own needs. His family and friends were amazed by the change in his character; he just could not come to terms with the backbiting, private deals and hostility which seemed to go hand in hand with public office. He maintains that he did not do a very good job, that he upset a lot of people, mainly through his naivety, and that he made a lot of enemies by speaking out on behalf of his fellow competitors. He recounts the story of the 1988 Plenary conference in Brazil, where the FIM had circulated a list of proposed changes to the regulations to all delegates. Taking his position seriously, he approached all the sidecar drivers with a questionnaire to ascertain their views on the proposals, compiling a list of their responses and working out the percentages in favour of the changes and those against. When the Plenary conference discussed the proposal to alter the points scoring system, Steve stood up and announced that he had taken a poll of the drivers and that 80 per cent of them were in favour of retaining the existing system. So he was naturally horrified when he was verbally attacked by Sito Pons, who told Steve that the committee had reached a totally different decision during discussions in the coffee-break, where all such important decisions were made! Steve had not been invited to this coffee morning and had not been told what the solo riders and teams wanted, so yet again he had managed to upset and annoy a large percentage of the Grand Prix community. He left the meeting saying to his wife Karen, 'Now nobody is speaking to me, you've really done it this time, Webbo, they all hate you!'

During the 18 months that he represented the sidecar riders on the FIM committees, Steve never became comfortable with the political chicanery, private meetings to fix decisions, and the change from hostility in the meetings to backslapping bonhomie outside them. He eventually resigned from his position on the FIM; his machine preparation had suffered; it had adversely affected his riding; he had alienated his fellow competitors and officials, and despite his untiring work and self-sacrifice, the plight of the sidecar crews was no better than before. No-one else stepped forward to replace him; they were all too busy to get involved! Subsequently, the FIM decided to terminate the practice of having riders' representatives on the road race committee. Nowadays the riders are represented by IRTA or by the recently founded ISRA, the International Sidecar Riders Association, who have Lee Van Damm, Egbert Streuer's team manager, as their spokesman.

'All this was weighing me down, as well as Biland's excellent performances in the first three Grand Prix. Biland had taken on the experienced Harold Bartols to look after his Krauser engine and he seemed to be invincible. Our next round was at Assen and I'm afraid it proved to be the same old story; Biland sweeping to victory as if his outfit was on rails, and Tony and I battling with a jumping sprocket,' moans Steve.

The race at Assen saw Rolf claim his 50th Grand Prix victory and an 18 point lead in the Championship. 'Our only hope of keeping the title,' comments Webster, 'was to hope that Rolf would have a few breakdowns in the forthcoming rounds. He seemed unbeatable.'

It seemed as if the rain would never stop in 1988. When the GP riders arrived at Spa-Francorchamps in Belgium, the bad weather appeared relentless. The conditions caused both Biland and Webster to spin at La Source, although Biland had a big enough lead to recover and speed on to the chequered flag, causing Webster to drop from second to third. He did, however, manage to regain second as Streuer had to retire with a cracked cylinder head. There was some happiness around, nevertheless, amongst the sidecar teams, and Derek Jones and Peter Brown were full of the joys despite the weather. Not only had they won enough money by their finish (fifth) in Holland to continue their unsponsored attack on the Championship, but Jones had his first rostrum place in six years, coming in third when Michel and Fresc spun out at La Source on the final lap.

A change in the weather occurred for the next Grand Prix in France, and a visit to the sunny 3.61-mile Paul Ricard circuit. It was the same old story, though, with an extra sting in the tail, as Biland smashed the lap record previously held by Webster and Hewitt. The old record, held since 1986, of 2min 07.46sec at 101.97mph, was replaced by Biland's and Waltisperg's 103.78mph lap in 2min 05.23sec. Biland had now clocked up six wins in a row.

'We just could not match his power out of the corners,' sighs Steve; 'at least knowing how this all ended up, it isn't quite as bad talking about it, but by this stage of the season we just didn't know what we had to do to beat Rolf! I even began to get psychologically beaten by him, I couldn't beat him – that was it. I'd say to my dad and to Karen, "I'll never beat him again, that's it now, I just can't beat Biland". I was developing quite a thing about him. With the British GP coming up, I was feeling more and more stressed.'

With yet another second place under his belt, Steve came home to York to prepare for the British Grand Prix, the one that he must win. 'I always worry about my concentration at Donington,' confesses Steve, 'I know the circuit so well that it's almost a disadvantage. I could relax and drift off course. But I must force myself to concentrate, I must win!'

Webster had Donington all worked out, so the question was whether he could break the spell of Biland at the British Grand Prix on a scorching Sunday, August 7, 1988. A crowd of 81,000 were holding their breath to see if Webster could power his LCR over the line for a repeat of the previous year's exciting British victory. Flags and banners were waving patriotically, Union flags with Webster's and Hewitt's names emblazoned on them waved in the breeze. The atmosphere was electric. The pair qualified second; it looked like a repeat of the other six rounds, with Biland and Waltisperg on pole with nearly a two-second lead. The first 10 laps were an epic struggle, Biland brilliant as always and Streuer up there giving it his best. In front of their television screens millions of people were yelling themselves hoarse and willing the Yorkshireman to pull it off. The lead constantly swapped between Biland, Webster and Streuer, then Egbert dropped out of the frame with a blistered rear tyre so Biland and Webster were left to battle it out to the flag.

The lead changed constantly. Steve led for three laps and then on lap 15 Biland powered past. Webster pulled in front again a lap later, and on lap 18 Biland re-took command. To say the crowd was going wild would be a vast understatement! On lap 21 at the Old Hairpin, Steve and Tony seized the lead again. They were not going to lose this now. With Herculean effort, Webster and Hewitt turned up the power and finished with a two-second lead. The lap of honour took over 30 minutes with Sports Minister Colin Moynihan on board. A wonderful and unforgettable day for British motorsport. But friend Biland at least had the consolation of claiming the lap record and was still in front overall by 21 points.

There remained only two rounds for the title to be retained. The next round was the following week, in Sweden, so there was not even time to deliberate. In 1987 Webster had clinched the World title at Anderstorp; this year it was Webster's aim to stop Rolf Biland doing the same.

Biland qualified badly: fourth, his worst position all season. Steve and Tony on the other hand qualified on pole. The Egloffs, who had qualified second, led away at the green light but it wasn't long before Rolf pushed his way through. Webster was determined that he wasn't going to be beaten, the victory at Donington having revitalized his confidence. Biland got into the lead, but Webster amazed him by passing him on the straight. Biland clawed back into the lead, and with two laps to go it was neck-and-neck. Steve outbraked Biland into the infamous right-hander and raced to the flag, one second ahead of the Swiss ace. Everything hung on the last round at Brno.

'Realistically,' says Steve, 'I realized that I had little chance of retaining the world title. All we could do was get out there and try our very best. Rolf had got an 18 point lead and all he had to do was finish 14th or above to clinch the title. Our chances were not very good.'

In order to save money, Steve and Tony did not travel home in between the Swedish Grand Prix and the Brno round as there was only a fortnight between them. So the duo went to Zandvoort to take part in an International race. During practice, disaster struck as Tony fell out of the outfit and injured his shoulder. As if Webster hadn't got enough to worry about, he now had to search for a stand-in passenger. Paul Atkinson very kindly lent his passenger, Gavin Simmons, to Steve, and Paul used a Dutch passenger.

The Czechoslovakian Grand Prix would be Gavin's second ride with the World Champion and only his third Grand Prix. The new couple qualified in second position, with Biland on pole. They got off to a cracking start, closely followed by the Egloffs and Streuer. Biland was happy to stroll along in fourth; his victory in the World

Championship almost assured. The race progressed and suddenly Mick Webster, in the pit lane, could not believe his eyes! Biland was slowing down, he had dropped to ninth, but he'd have to drop to 15th and Webster win, to lose the title. He limped on, but became slower and slower. Biland and Waltisperg coasted to a halt on the start and finish line and there were still four laps to go. Biland must have been praying that Streuer would beat Webster, in which case the title would be safe. Mick Webster was on his hands and knees, reaffirming that there is a God after all! Biland's Krauser had stuck in third gear, so their race was run. Mick's heart was in his mouth; he hardly dared watch.

Stand-in passenger Gavin Simmons was doing a great job, but the pair were oblivious to what had happened. As far as they were concerned, Streuer was chasing hard, and Webster and Simmons had to keep him at bay because a win for Streuer was a win for Biland. The last four laps lasted an eternity. Streuer was climbing all over Webster, but Webster slammed the door shut in his face. They crossed the line with half a second to spare! It was a dream come true! 'It wasn't until it was all over that we really realized what had happened. We had thought the yellow outfit was the Egloffs. It was wonderful.'

No doubt a lot of journalists were very quickly having to rewrite their race reports because the unexpected had happened. Tony Hewitt, back home in Yorkshire, raised a glass in celebration. The World crown was to stay in England; the nation saluted Steve, Tony and Gavin.

'I didn't expect to win the World Championship at Brno,' reflects Steve, looking back on 1988. 'I knew I had little chance of retaining the title. Gavin and I tried our best and were rewarded in the most perfect of ways. When 1988 is mentioned, I think of that moment in Czecho, and of the win at Donington when thousands of people swarmed on to the track to congratulate us. That is an afternoon that Tony and I will never forget. Sidecar racing is all about teamwork, and I had a fantastic team. I can't begin to thank my dad enough for all his hard work and dedication; to Mary Smith, our team co-ordinator, who has made so many sacrifices to support the team, and of course Tony and Gavin, who are superb passengers. You can't get anywhere in racing without a good team and I'd got the best. At the end of 1988 I also had the conviction that my team would be working at full tilt throughout the winter to prepare to win the championship for the third year in a row.'

1989 was to begin with a different venue for the sidecar teams, a trip to the Laguna Seca circuit in America. The Grand Prix season was already underway for the 500cc competitors. They had been to Japan and to Australia, but Webster was not envious of these extra rounds. 'The journey from Australia to Laguna Seca must be a killer,' he remarks. 'There wouldn't be enough time to recover from the travelling and crossing the date line. We were happy to go straight to Laguna Seca and even happier when we found out we'd accidentally won a day's exclusive sidecar testing!'

This was one occasion when Cinderella really did get to the ball. The sidecar teams arrived bright-eyed and bushy-tailed at the Californian circuit. The 'big boys' were already getting very wound up at the thought of visiting Laguna. They'd had bad experiences there the previous year, finding the track resurfaced with the wrong mixture of tarmac and the organizers and marshals delightfully laid back. The chair contingent, on the other hand, had no previous experiences to cloud their judgment and were looking forward to racing outside of Europe.

An industrial dispute caused the 500cc machines to be delayed at Phillip Island, and in order to be fair on the testing front, it was agreed that no 500cc team should test until Friday. This left all day Thursday for the sidecars to practice. 'You couldn't help but smile,' grins Webster, 'a bit of role reversal for a change.'

The circuit at Laguna Seca has a notorious section called the Corkscrew, and Webster attacked this with gusto! 'I was impressed with all the track actually,' says Steve, 'the surface had been improved since 1989 and we found it quite acceptable, although there wasn't much grip. Yes, there is a lack of run-off areas and it could be tricky if you went off and had to be attended to at certain parts of the track. We'd heard timing might also be a problem, so Lee Van Dam set up a computer for lap times in the paddock, and this worked perfectly. The Corkscrew was not as horrendous as we'd heard, but it certainly proved tricky. It was very hard work for Tony, as he had to change positions just as you drop over the edge, but he always was a smooth and precise passenger, and he coped brilliantly. His timing was superb and I always tried to get the line right.'

The Egloffs put in a memorable performance at Laguna. They were second in first practice and eventually claimed pole. Then they flew, to claim a 1min 32sec lap.

So it was back to the pits to consult with Mick in order to make adjustments to catch the Egloffs. 'We weren't used to left-handed circuits,' remembers Steve, 'and we also had this grip problem. The new tarmac was slippery and dusty. We altered the suspension and hoped that it would do the trick, and we decided not to go for soft compound tyres.'

The lights changed and the race was underway. Markus and Urs shot off the line. 'They were off like bats out of hell,' claims Webster; 'I didn't think we could catch them. I usually try to pace myself to look after my tyres, and although Avons are excellent at coming back on song after they've heated up and then cooled a little, some tyres have had it once they are really hot. Luckily for us, the Egloffs were too hard on the brakes, and although they managed a well deserved rostrum place, we pipped them in the end. Alain Michel claimed second and Markus and Urs were third. A superb start to a new season!'

The Grand Prix circus rolled on to Spain and Italy, but without the inclusion of the sidecar contingent. Meanwhile, preparation was underway back at Flawith to collect another 20 points at Hockenheim. 'I knew Eggy (Streuer) had a new passenger for Germany and I wondered how they'd make out. Gerald De Haas is much smaller and lighter than Schneiders, but it actually worked out startlingly well, and it was Egbert who was my arch rival for the lead, my old pal Rolf having lost his ignition rotor. I had a coming together with the Lucky Strike outfit at the chicane – my fault as we had gone into the chicane too fast to try to stop Egbert, we rather overcooked it!' grins Steve. Despite this, the British pair claimed victory, unbeaten so far in 1989, but Austria was to change this.

'Perhaps I'd got a little too confident,' muses Webster, 'I was on pole, with a practice time of 1min 25.79sec and I knew I could win. I intended to make a break for it at the start so I'd no other outfits in my slipstream. The starter seemed to hold us for an eternity, so I might as well blame him. Nothing to do with Webbo over enthusiasm, you know! I'd cooked the clutch; it took me two goes to get off the line.

'I pitted at the end of the second lap and my dad frantically poured water all over the clutch. Austria is only 2.636 miles long and we were lapped before we emerged from the pits. We went like mad. If ever there was a race where I can say we gave it everything, this was it. We smashed the lap record and got up to 15th place. This was the hardest Championship point of my life! I held on to my lead by 2 points, with Masato Kumano just behind me in the Championship table. The winner that day though, was an elated Rolf Biland!'

'We didn't go to Yugoslavia, as there wasn't a round for us there. As it turned out, all the lads who were there were very depressed, because whilst the teams were at Rijeka, news came that both Phil Mellor and Steve Henshaw had sustained fatal injuries at the Isle of Man TT. This brought the fatalities that year to five. Everyone was labouring under a cloud of "Is it really worth it?". Phil and Steve were great lads; we were all very saddened. I dread news of the TT; it's always bad and you know next year it'll be bad again.'

The next outing for team Webster was to Holland at the famous Assen Speed Week. This is a week when it pays to be Dutch. Mick Webster had considered painting a false Dutch-sounding name on the van to ensure getting out of the country unscathed! After Steve and Tony's resounding victory at Assen, locals attacked the bike, kicking it and swearing – 'Just like those early races at Carnaby all over again,' laughs Steve!

Webster and Streuer had battled all the way. Having qualified on grid three, they soon claimed second place, Egbert in the lead and Steve battling hard. Biland, who had been on pole, dropped back with numerous problems. At the last chicane before the start and finish straight, the Dutchman went on to the grass and Webster roared to victory. Webster got a weak round of applause from the crowd and a resounding victory yell from the satellite viewers back at home. Anyone doubtful about parting with £60 for a three-day British GP ticket had now had their minds made up!

There were two rounds to go before Donington, one of which was the rain-soaked Belgian Grand Prix. Here the spray was so bad that Webster, who waterskied home to second place, had no idea that Biland was right on his tail. However, Egbert set the score right for his fans by beating Steve. 'He is brilliant in the wet,' comments Steve, 'he drives like it isn't even raining. He took an early lead and used the advantage of a clear road ahead and good visibility. Well, not good, it was torrential, but he did have visibility free from the spray of another competitor. We had been on pole, but I'd missed a couple of gears and Eggy and Gerald got away. I was frozen, what a day!'

Steve had accepted second at Spa, just glad to be off the bike and back in the warmth of the van to get dry at last. He also had to accept second at Paul Ricard. 'I'll have to moan about the weather again here actually,' quips Webster, 'I was too cold and too wet at Spa; at Paul Ricard it was scorchingly hot and the tyres were suffering. I was sliding around all over the place, but as we had a good lead in the points, I thought I'd better settle for second and at least finish. 'Streuer was my biggest threat Championship points-wise and he'd made a disastrous start. He ended up third, with Rolf taking the laurels. We still had a nine point lead, so although it's great to win, I was beginning to get quite sensible. Worrying isn't it?!'

At last the day of Webster's favourite GP had arrived, the one he most wanted to win, the event that fans wait all year to come to and book their holidays around. Like pilgrims going to Mecca they flock in their tens of thousands to the lovely Leicestershire circuit, to wave their Union flags and bellow until they are hoarse, longing for a British victory, longing for Steve to make it three wins in a row. Webster and Hewitt had a following of fans bigger than ever before, and Brown Brothers had gone to town with a hospitality venture which put the 500 riders in the shade. Leggy promotions girls sold Webster and Hewitt umbrellas to eager fans, and British hearts beat under 'Go for it Webbo' emblazoned tee shirts. Redgate Corner was completely taken over by a huge marquee provided by Brown Brothers; the sidecar world had never seen anything like it. Steve was even asked, 'Why if Brown's could do all this, were they supporting chairs? This was 500 material!' Mike Trimby was reeling in shocked amazement as this mighty display overlooked the Castrol and Yamaha hospitality units.

They did justice to the efforts of Ron and Gordon Brown by winning the race for the third year in succession. Unlike previous years where it had been a battle, Webster zoomed into a clear one second lead, and he was consistently under the lap record.

It was a great day for the team, the sponsors and, of course, the delighted fans.

The next round at Anderstorp was a fantastic battle between Rolf Biland and Alain Michel. Alain loves to race hard against Rolf. They are both very talented, thinking drivers. Even though Alain came in second, he still labels it as one of his favourite races. Steve and Tony having been on pole, cruised in, in third place. 'We still had to finish in Czecho, to win the Championship,' remarks Steve. 'This is the sort of time when all your plans can go sadly awry!'

On then to August 27, 1989, the make or break race for Webster and Hewitt to make it three in a row. Biland and Waltisperg claimed pole and the British pair were second. Webster made a good start and led at the end of the first lap; Streuer and De Haas were pressuring them. 'It was all very hectic,' reflects Steve 'and the best thing to do was to ease off, drop back and stay out of trouble. The main thing was to finish. It was all happening up there ahead of us, with Alain Michel fighting for the lead, and the Egloffs and the Zurbruggs getting in the frame. I hung back. This was the hardest World Championship to get hold of. The first one had seemed straight forward, the second one was quite a surprise, but this was very different. The pressure was intense. We ended up in a comfortable third place with Streuer winning and the Egloffs close runners-up. It didn't matter that we were third, as the World crown was again in the bag!'

Steve and Tony were elated. The 145 points had assured them a third victory in a row, but once the celebrations were over, Steve Webster had changes to make. The fans did not realize that they were in fact witnessing the end of an era.

8

Trials and Tribulations

1990 saw the start of a new decade and a significant change in Steve Webster's life. The winter of 1989/90 was probably the most traumatic of Steve's career, and it was the foretaste of a season that was to turn his whole world around, bringing dispute, despair, disappointment and failure.

For eight years the partnership of Steve Webster and Tony Hewitt had carried all before them, winning at every level of the sport, from the early days in the British Championship to the heady days of three successive World Championship titles. When Steve announced that the partnership was breaking up, the press had a field day, fuelling speculation of a rift between the two champions, searching for some hidden reason, some dark secret that had caused the break-up. The constant searching and probing by the press did nothing to help the growing antagonism felt by the two people central to the drama. It certainly didn't get to the truth behind the break-up, and to this day the real facts have never been explained.

To search out the reasons for the split in the most successful partnership in sidecar history, it is necessary to go back in time to the period when Steve was involved in the FIM as the rider's representative. For the first time in their relationship Steve and Tony started to have major disagreements. These centered around Steve's involvement in the running of the sport and his subsequent distraction from preparing the machine. Steve's preoccupation with the responsibilities of the position at the FIM was making him irritable and unapproachable. Naturally his close friends and family backed away from provoking confrontation. As the relationship changed Steve began to form the impression that Tony was not as committed to chasing the World Championship as he had been in previous seasons. He mistook Tony's reticence for lack of motivation, but did have a genuine concern for Tony's inability to conduct long periods of testing due to tiredness.

It is important to understand the Webster character when looking at this situation. Steve's greatest failing at this time was his inability to approach Tony directly in order to talk through the problem. He just could not bring himself to upset his friend of the last eight years by raising the subject of Tony's continuing commitment. Steve reflects, 'One of my mistakes at the time was to drop hints about how I felt, and hope that Tony would realize the seriousness of the situation. If we could have sorted our differences out, things may well have been resolved. I used to say things like, "I'll be making a lot of changes in this team come next season". I wanted Tony to follow this up and ask about these changes, but he never did. I guess he knew what I was getting at but he didn't want to face it.' Hewitt never approached Steve to sort out the problems that were beginning to come between them, problems which were threatening to reduce their competitiveness, and Steve never came straight out with the root of the problem.

Throughout 1989 the impression that Tony's enthusiasm was waning grew in Steve's mind. He was also aware that he really needed a passenger with some mechanical aptitude to help in the area of machine preparation, and that ideally this passenger would be a full-time member of the team. Tony worked for British Rail, and although his employers were very understanding and tolerant of his need to have time off for testing and racing, Steve knew that he could not ask him to give up work completely. After all, Tony was 38 years of age with a wife and family to support, and Hewitt was beginning to show his age, having less and less stamina, particularly when intensive tyre testing was called for.

So, in Steve's thinking, the way ahead was clear: he would find a younger passenger who would be willing to take at least a year off work and who could help with the mechanical side of the operation. This would allow Tony to retire gracefully without any of the soul searching that is always so difficult for a racer contemplating retirement from the sport.

If Webster and Hewitt had been able to discuss their problems and Steve's suggestions for the future, they may have been able to avoid the acrimony and bad publicity which followed. By trying to avoid a conflict with his friend and partner of so many campaigns, Steve managed to destroy a friendship and start a controversy which would provide pages of speculation in the press for months to come. Today the two are barely on speaking terms. Steve says 'Tony is a brilliant passenger and a smashing bloke, but we don't get together socially nowdays.' The friendship and camaraderie of the partnership has gone, making an unsatisfactory end to nearly a decade of dominance in sidecar racing. 'I'll never forget the day when it all came to a head,' says Steve, 'I'd been going to discuss Tony's role, and all through the season I was trying to pick my moment. In some ways I was afraid to raise the subject, in case I demotivated Tony. We were such a good pairing and I knew we could clinch the title again, but I didn't want to sour things.' Yet Steve had to make the change for the reasons mentioned earlier: a full-time partner and a younger man. 'How could I tell my friend something I knew he didn't want to hear? Tony kept saying he wanted to retire, but it's hard to quit when you are at the top. I also wanted to give Tony time to find another ride, if he wanted one.'

My dad was less than sympathetic at the way I was delaying the discussion. Looking back I can see that all the procrastination was helping no-one. I was avoiding facing the music. I tried various tactics, such as on one night when Tony went out for a drink. Here I tried my usual line about changes, but we were having far too good a time to go into all this then. We did get on very, very well. I lost a great friend when we finally did split.

'The season was over, we had won the Championship for the third time in a row, a marvellous achievement. We were both due to go on holiday. I knew I must tell Tony before he went away, but then I might ruin his well earned rest. I was in turmoil. Tony was getting very excited about a deal that he was working on to acquire promotional clothing, teeshirts, jackets etc. There is very little available advertising sidecar teams and fans often query this, and this was a great idea, but I couldn't let Tony go ahead and pay a fortune for all this gear when I intended to replace him. The garments he'd organized were very tasteful and well made; they were ideal for promoting us. Tony was always better at trying to get us noticed than I was, but I had to step in. We'd been doing an "appearance" at the York Show and had ended up in the bar for an end of day drink. I knew I couldn't tell Tony in the bar, he needed to be told privately. Heaven knows, I owed him that; in a place where he could walk away or where we could talk alone without being under scrutiny. I'd lain awake at nights and considered all options. I'd never tell him by letter as that was the coward's way out, and same goes for a phone call. With either of our families present it would have been inappropriate as we were all such friends, so it had to be just the two of us, out of the public gaze. Tony was enjoying his drink and again talking about this clothing deal. I couldn't let him spend his own money on this well-intentioned, but fruitless venture, so I said, "Tony, I'm going now and I've got something to say, can you walk to the car with me?" I'm sure he knew what was coming. You can't be in a close relationship like we were and not learn to read each other's minds.

'We got to the car but Tony's enthusiasm about this deal was so difficult to dampen – yet I had to tell him. "Look Tony" – I blurted it out at last – "about next year. I'm changing the team. This isn't Steve Webster your friend talking now, now I've got my management hat on. I need a younger passenger and one who can take a year off work for intensive testing". Tony looked so wounded. "Why?" he said. I explained that I wanted to go on winning and that I was aware of Tony's tiredness. I didn't want to risk our safety. I didn't want him to give up a good career for the racing. He'd got a wife and daughter to consider and he was approaching 40. Tony was really hurt, and no wonder. There's nothing I can say to lighten up this part of the story. I felt gutted. We both did. I was anxious that at least we were in the car park and Tony could walk away and still have his self-esteem.

'Just at this moment, who should pop along but an eager fan, wanting our autographs. "Can you sign this?" she asked brightly. "Oh, you don't want my name", said Tony. The poor girl thought she'd got the wrong pair. "Aren't you Webster and Hewitt?" she queried, nearly as embarrassed as we were. "Yes, love", I said; "Look, I'm afraid Tony has just been told some bad news, go back into the show and I'll sort you out a poster later". The poor miffed girl went away and we stood there suddenly alienated. It was rather like getting divorced. It's impossible to describe accurately what a wrench this was.

'I powered away in my car to a motocross track and jumped straight on my bike and pounded relentlessly round and round until I was physically exhausted. If anyone had treated me like I just treated Tony, I don't know what I'd have done. This was one of the worst days of my life.'

Financially, it would have been prudent for the household names of Webster and Hewitt to stay together, even if they had not won any more races because as a pair they were very attractive to sponsors. 'I wish we were still friends,' says Steve, 'I haven't changed from those halcyon days when we got on so well. The public expect us to be different with each other, but I don't think a relationship like ours can ever be totally eradicated. I hope not.'

The man chosen to replace Tony Hewitt was Gavin Simmons, a 29 year old mechanical fitter at Rowntrees factory in York. He had started his motorsport career driving a rally car, ably partnered by his wife, Julie. Steve and Gavin had met at technical college, whilst both on day release, training to be fitters. Gavin is a year younger than Steve so they were not in the same group at college, but they were eager to spend coffee-breaks together discussing racing. On Fridays they travelled back to Rowntrees together to collect their wages, and it was on one of these journeys back to work after college that the basis of one of today's most famous sports pairings came about. Gavin had begun sidecar racing at club level with a friend called Keith Blacker. Simmons was keen to try a faster bike, but Keith did not have the finances available to progress beyond club racing level. Steve put him in touch with Paul Atkinson, a well-known rider in the York area, who was planning to contest the European series. Steve described Gavin as a perfectionist; whatever he takes on, be it racing or DIY, he has to have it spot on! Gavin partnered Paul for a year and Paul had loaned him to Steve on that occasion at Zandvoort after Tony Hewitt had been injured. The pair worked well together and after their inaugural outing in Holland they teamed up again a week later, Hewitt still being incapacitated, and went on to win the Czechoslovakian Grand Prix.

Steve had verbally agreed that Hewitt would continue as passenger in 1989, but Tony had expressed his intention to retire in the not too distant future. Although Gavin had relatively little World Championship experience, Steve now knew who he would like to take the most coveted seat in sidecar racing. Gavin's employers, Rowntree-Mackintosh, had agreed to give him a year's leave of absence from work to enable him to mount a concerted effort to lift the World crown.

The season started in America at the Laguna Seca circuit in California. The new pairing gelled straight away, and although they were outpowered by Alain Michel and Simon Birchall, they contested the lead in the early stages and finished in a comfortable second place.

Round two of the Championship was held at Jerez in Spain and was a significant milestone in Steve's career. This was to be his 50th Grand Prix and he celebrated it in totally dominant style, leading from lights to flag and breaking the course record on his way to his 12th Grand Prix victory. This win pushed Steve into the joint lead of the World Championship with Alain Michel. The season appeared to be getting off to a good start. The acrimony of the winter was behind him, his new passenger was settling into the team and things were looking good!

Round three, at Misano in Italy – and disaster struck. Steve had a large accident in practice and fractured his shoulder. In considerable pain he ignored medical advice and decided to race, but wasn't sure if he could last the distance in the heat. Amazingly he managed to take the lead early in the race, but was forced to ease his pace as the pain increased, and had to settle for second place behind an on-form Rolf Biland. Chief rival Alain Michel had mechanical problems late in the race and had to retire with just three of the 26 laps remaining, so Steve and Gavin went into a clear lead in the World Championship.

Despite being in pain from the injured shoulder, Steve strolled to victory at the Nurburgring in Germany, the fourth round of the series. All his main rivals ran into problems and he increased his points advantage in the Championship. With a second place in the torrential rain in Austria and third at Rijeka in Yugoslavia, Steve and Gavin went to the famous Assen circuit in Holland with a 31 point advantage over their nearest rivals with half the season completed.

Assen was the turning point of the year for several reasons. The main factor influencing the outcome of the Championship was about to unfold. For some time Steve had been concerned by the lateness of his sponsorship payments from his major backers, Brown Group International. His finances were at an all-time low and he desperately needed the input from his sponsors to maintain his challenge for the title. 'My concerns about Brown's were fuelled by a rumour I heard in the paddock at Assen,' explains Steve. 'I telephoned my wife to tell her that there were rumours that Browns were in financial difficulties, to which she said that confirmation that they had gone bust had been on the news! I wasted no time in telephoning Browns, only to be told that, "No", I couldn't speak to Gordon Brown and that the receivers were now in control. The receiver asked me who I was, and I told him that I was ringing from the paddock at Assen in Holland and I was sponsored by Browns. His reply was not exactly very encouraging: "If I were you, lad, whilst you're over there I'd look for another sponsor. When it comes to creditors you'll be right at the back of the queue!"'

At this point Brown Group owed Steve £70,000 in sponsorship payments. Steve had already spent most of this sum in anticipation of receiving it, so he was seriously in debt. He needed money to continue, and there was no sign of any fairy godmother on the horizon. He did not know if he could carry on. In a few short minutes his whole life appeared to have changed from being comfortably in the lead of the World Championship with an understanding and supportive sponsor, to being out in the cold, with a race to run, new parts needed and no money at all. Worse still, he had borrowed heavily in anticipation of receiving the money owed to him under his sponsorship contract!

Whether it was the pressures of losing his backing that was weighing so heavily on his mind, or whether he just made a fundamental mistake, even Steve does not know what made him slip the clutch for too long at the start of the race. Whatever the reason, he overheated the clutch and for the first time in the last 40 Grands Prix he had failed to finish!

'I'm sure you can imagine how I felt when I was packing up the equipment at Assen,' says Steve. 'Most people were keeping well out of the way. What could anyone say? Only a miracle could save me now.' If anyone else other than Steve Webster had been in this position, the outcome would almost certainly have been different. However, the scenario at Assen was one situation where Webster's amenable personality and pleasant disposition saved the day. 'I'd noticed this big bloke in biker gear hanging around in the pit garage,' explains Steve. He seemed very interested in what was going on. I was removing my Brown's stickers at the time and my dad was saying, "Leave them on", but I thought it was counter-productive to appear sponsored when you're not! The biker watched for a while, asked one or two questions about the bike and what I was doing with the stickers, and then he went away. He came back later with Paul Mottram, who works for our helmet suppliers, Levoir. I was aghast when Paul introduced the man as Roland Munch, head of Munch industries, who wanted to help me out with some sponsorship.'

At Spa-Francorchamps, for the Belgium Grand Prix, Steve's problems worsened. He lost a comfortable second place on the last lap when the gearbox disintegrated, finally coasting over the line to take sixth place. He had known that he needed to replace the parts in the gearbox but his sponsorship problems had prevented him from doing so as he just didn't have the money to do the job properly. Of greater significance was the fact that his 31 point lead in the Championship had been eroded to just five points in the space of two races.

Webster bounced back at the French Grand Prix at Le Mans, scoring a confidence-boosting victory, his third of the year. Alain Michel's engine failed in the oppressive heat whilst he was leading in his home Grand Prix. Steve's win in France extended his lead in the championship to 21 points over Egbert Streuer, with Michel a further four points adrift.

Next it was the turn of Donington Park, home of the British Grand Prix and a crucial race for all the Championship contenders. Steve had attracted additional sponsorship from the satellite television company BSB and was anxious to secure a good result in front of his local fans and sponsors. In qualifying, he and Gavin did all that their adoring supporters could have asked for, scorching round the 2½-mile Leicestershire circuit at record speeds to grab pole position for the 24-lap, 60-mile race. They then threw all that hard work away by making a dreadful start, bogging down as the lights turned to green and being swamped by over half the field before the first corner. This poor start was probably a legacy of Steve's clutch-burning getaway at Assen. Since that race he had been over-cautious with the clutch, and in making sure that he didn't slip it he allowed the engine revs to die, so that consequently the machine just would not accelerate away from the grid. In trying to make up for the fiasco at the start, they were involved in a heavy collision with another competitor whilst disputing the racing line at the chicane. The impact caused extensive damage to the two-stroke engine's critical exhaust system. With the exhaust flattened and the engine unable to rev, they had no alternative but to head slowly to the pits and retirement. The machine was too badly damaged to continue.The scream of the high-revving two-stroke engines was drowned by the moan of disappointment from the 100,000 strong crowd as they realized that their hero was out of the race. As Egbert Streuer cruised to victory, many fans were already making for the exits, their interest in the race having evaporated along with Webster's World Championship aspirations.

In the Championship standings Steve now led Streuer by a single point and Michel by eight points. In the last five weeks his seemingly invincible lead in the title chase had disappeared, his resources were stretched to breaking point, his competitors had a definite advantage in straight-line performance and he was still very heavily in debt.

Donington effectively decided the outcome of the Championship, despite the fact that there were still two rounds to go, in Sweden and Czechoslovakia. It was Steve's failure to score at the British round that ultimately cost him the title because at the end of the year Alain Michel and Simon Birchall won the World Championship by just two points from Egbert Streuer and Gerald de Haas while Webster and Simmons were third, just one point behind Streuer.

It was a year to forget: the dispute and bad feeling with Hewitt; a bad accident at Misano; the loss of his faithful and generous sponsors. A period of unreliability had arrived after he had driven 40 consecutive Grands Prix without a single retirement; he was massively in debt and had lost the World title to his close friend Alain Michel. It was time to rebuild, a time to put the past behind him, to look to the future and to set about regaining his World Championship.

Despite all the disappointments, there had been some high points: the three race wins, the chance meeting with Roland

Munch which promised so much for the future, other potential sponsors who were willing to fill the void left by Browns, and his unfailing popularity with the fans. The media had supported him more in his adversity than they had when he was in funds, and there was still the round of celebrity appearances, charity shows and on-circuit demonstrations to look forward to, which were always fun.

One of the pleasant side effects of Steve's continuing success and growing popularity was the increasing demand to experience the thrills of sidecar racing from the hot seat. These requests came not only from members of the press, anxious to impress their readers, but also from members of the public and even from some solo riders!

One of the first solo stars to experience the passenger's perch on the Webster outfit was long-time friend and often outspoken critic of the 'wobbly wheelers', Roger Burnett. After two laps of Donington Park Roger was forced to eat his words, being amazed at the levels of braking, acceleration and cornering of which the three-wheelers were capable. He said that although the sidecar outfit was not as fast as his solo machine in a straight line, in every other aspect of performance the chair was awesome. It obviously required enormous levels of skill and courage from both the rider and passenger to get the ultimate performance out of one. Roger has never criticized the sidecar racers from that day, although he has been known to question their sanity on occasions, having had firsthand experience of what is required to stay aboard a well-driven outfit at racing speeds!

Steve admits to making several errors of judgment when taking inexperienced passengers for a quick lap of a racing circuit. He says that it is particularly difficult knowing just how fast to go, particularly when he has a journalist in the chair. Does he go slowly so as not to frighten him and then risk the journalist writing that it is no big deal to race a sidecar as they aren't that quick! Alternatively, he can go for it and run the risk of frightening the poor soul out of his skin, or even worse, throwing him off the outfit and injuring him.

One of his earliest errors came at Brands Hatch, where John Webb would not pay any starting or appearance money. He would, however, pay Steve to do some PR work for the circuit. This PR exercise involved him in taking a journalist from Radio Kent for a few laps of the track. After kitting out the radio presenter with leathers, gloves, boots and helmet, and making sure that his microphone and recording equipment worked, they set out for a slow lap of the circuit. Webster had explained before they set off that he would do one slow lap, at the end of which he would look round at his passenger. If everything was all right the journalist was to nod his head, then Steve would go a bit faster on the next lap. If, on the other hand, the journalist was not enjoying his ride, he was to shake his head, in which case Steve would pull into the pits. At the end of the first lap Steve looked back at his passenger as arranged but there was no movement from the man from Radio Kent; he certainly wasn't shaking his head. So with another quick glance to make sure, Steve opened the throttles and proceeded to do a fairly quick lap of the 1.2-mile circuit.

Steve realized that something was wrong as he peeled off into the pit lane at the end of the lap. 'I could feel a strange vibration which wasn't coming from the machine. As I came to a halt I saw the journalist's helmet alongside me. He appeared to be growling and pulling faces. I thought that the radio man was about to attack me, but luckily before the situation could develop he was pulled off the machine by a colleague. Another reporter took his place to be whisked around the circuit. When I returned to the pits after several laps, the man from Radio Kent had calmed down a bit, although he was as white as a sheet and shaking! As I climbed off the bike and removed my helmet, the journalist's colleague came rushing over to me saying, "just listen to this – it's hysterical!" The tape recording started calmly enough: "I am just setting off, on the passenger compartment of Steve Webster's World Championship-winning sidecar outfit, for a lap of the Brands Hatch circuit", but soon the dialogue deteriorated to – "Oh dear – Oh my God, this is unbelievable – Christ! What's he doing now? – Oh God, he's looking round at me – For God's sake look where you're going". Finally the tape recorder spewed out a series of oaths and blasphemies, as fear completely overcame the poor unfortunate!'

Steve says that the chap was cursing constantly, threatening physical harm to him if he didn't stop at once. Steve had no way of knowing this as the noise from the high-revving two-stroke engine completely drowned the journalist's cries for help!

On another occasion Steve was carrying out some work for the BBC's *Top Gear* programme, taking presenter and car racing driver Tiff Needell for some laps of Lincolnshire's Cadwell Park circuit, with cameras mounted on the bike. During a break in filming Webster was approached by two members of the *Motor Cycle News* road test team, Chris Dabbs and Olly Duke, who were at the circuit track-testing a large road bike. They inquired if Steve would take them for a few laps of the circuit. Steve, as ever, was keen to oblige, but told them that they would have to clear it with the BBC producer as it was his show. The man from the BBC said it was OK between filming sessions and the plans were made. Steve would take first Chris and then Olly for two or three laps each, with a quick change-over between passengers, whilst the BBC were repositioning their cameras.

Steve explained his by now normal one slow lap, next one quicker procedure to the two *MCN* journalists before they set off. As Chris Dabbs was settling into position on the sidecar, Olly Duke came up to Steve and said, 'It's all right, he's done some passengering before.' Sure enough, Chris seemed to know what he was doing, leaning out on the corners and getting over the back wheel to aid traction onto the straights. Steve checked to make sure that Chris was OK at the end of the first lap, and being satisfied that he was, he put a really quick one in, getting very close to racing speed. Chris coped superbly and obviously enjoyed the experience, and at the end of that lap Steve pulled into the pits for his passengers to change over. As he got off Chris said to Steve, 'Great, loved it, by the way Olly's been on one before as well.'

At the end of the first lap, with Olly in the chair, Webster turned round to see his passenger leaning out in the correct manner and so thought, 'Ah, good, he knows what he's doing, I'll go for it.' Steve gave the outfit full bore up the hill out of Cadwell's tight hairpin and rocketed up towards Charlies, a long sweeping right-hand bend leading onto the main straight. Suddenly, exiting Charlies, the engine revs shot sky high and the bike pitched violently sideways. Steve knew at once what had happened – he'd lost his passenger! Fearing the worst, Steve fought to get the outfit back under control and managed to bring it to a halt a little way down the straight. He switched the engine off and turned round to look for his passenger. Of Olly there was no sign. 'Christ', thought Steve, 'I've killed him!' Then from amongst the piles of tyres and straw bales at the edge of the circuit the rumpled figure of Olly Duke started to emerge. He then began to run towards Steve. Steve did not know what to do, fearing that Olly would be so mad that he must be coming to have a go at him! Webster panicked, desperately wondering: 'How do I start the bike on my own?' He was just about to abandon the bike and make a run for it when he realized that Olly was laughing. In fact Olly was laughing so much that he could not speak, merely emitting high-pitched squeaking noises for several minutes. He finally managed to explain that he was not hurt, but that his new red leathers were ruined and that he had left a 20-yard red mark on the track surface before ploughing a huge furrow in the grass.

It later emerged that although Olly had had previous experience as a sidecar passenger, it was limited to a few laps on a vintage BMW-powered outfit, and that the enormous power of Steve's Krauser powered LCR machine had taken him totally by surprise! Many other would-be passengers have found that a modern Grand Prix outfit is a daunting proposition. Roger Marshall, a highly competitive and talented solo rider, found that his hands 'pumped up' after just a couple of laps so that he could no longer hang on.

At least all of Steve's guest passengers have fared better than one well-known journalist who persuaded Barry Brindley to take him round Mallory Park circuit at full racing speed. The journalist told Barry that he wanted to experience the machine at full bore, that he didn't want Barry to hold back at all. Barry took this literally and gave the machine full throttle in the anticipation that his passenger would be able to contribute the vital input required to keep the machine on the tarmac. Brindley's faith in his passenger's ability proved to be misguided, for not only could the poor journalist not perform the necessary antics to aid the outfit's cornering speed, but he also failed to keep a strong enough grip on the bucking and weaving machine, with the result that he was pitched off the outfit at high speed!

The journalist had told Barry, 'I want to know exactly what it's like to be on a sidecar,' but after the accident Barry was heard to remark, 'Now he knows what it's like to fall off a sidecar.' According to Barry the journalist wasn't badly hurt in the incident, although contemporary reports suggest that the man was admitted to a local hospital suffering from broken ankles, fingers and leg, not to mention extensive abrasions. This was not the first time that Barry Brindley had lost a guest passenger, and when Steve learnt that Barry and Darren Dixon were to join him in giving members of the public lifts around Donington Park at the 1991 Day of Champions, Webster insisted that he led the procession, on the grounds that he didn't want to be responsible for running over one of Barry's 'cast offs'!

Steve relates with relief that he has never actually ejected any members of the public from the chair. 'You have to be very careful when you are weighing up how to ride with a competition winner. I would hate to upset a fan or to put people off sidecar racing. It is not easy to put people into categories. You can obviously see if they are overweight or don't appear to be particularly fit, and in those instances I advise them to sit very still and HANG ON. However, what is hard to assess is how much of the real thrill of sidecar racing a person wants to experience. I cannot tell people what riding on a sidecar is like; it's like no other feeling. The unfortunate thing is that I've had people on the outfit who have looked forward to the ride and by the end of the lap have clearly hated it. Others are happy to sit there and be content to say they've been on Steve Webster's sidecar. Some are very keen to experience the stopping power, but are clearly surprised by the violent deceleration that the carbon-fibre brakes generate. I do try my utmost to tailor the ride to suit the person, but I wouldn't recommend it to those of a nervous disposition!'

9

A Bit on the Side

This chapter is not meant to be a definitive history of the racing sidecar outfit, but by chronicling Steve Webster's various machines, the progression from converted road-going machines of the early years to the sophisticated long-wheelbase 'worms' of today, can be seen.

Steve's first machine was a Fidderman chassis, originally built to house a twin-cylinder four-stroke Triumph engine. The Fidderman was a conventional outfit, similar to the motorcycle and sidecar combinations that our grandfathers used as everyday transport. The rider sat on the motorcycle frame, the passenger on a tubular outrigger bolted onto the main frame and had to lean out in front of the sidecar wheel to balance the machine on left-hand corners. The design of this outfit dated from the early 1960s and was hopelessly uncompetitive in this form, especially when compared with the newer purpose-built kneeler-type outfits which had been introduced into the sport. Webster modified his Fidderman chassis to make it look like the current machines of the day, even if it didn't quite work like one! The Triumph Twin was discarded and replaced with a three-cylinder two-stroke Suzuki engine, the old water-cooled 750 'kettle', which produced far more power than the antique British twin.

The Fidderman chassis was hacked about to the point where its creator would not have recognized it! Apeing the current fashions, Steve converted the machine to 'kneeler' specification, that is, where the rider kneels on the machine rather than sits in the saddle. This had the effect of pushing a lot more weight over the front wheel, making it heavy to steer and reducing the traction from the rear wheel. To help compensate for this, the sidecar wheel was moved forward, allowing the passenger to shift his weight backwards and lean out behind the sidecar wheel instead of in front of it. In racing parlance this meant that the chair was now a rear exit type instead of a front exit type.

Steve and his brother Kevin had a surprising amount of success with this much-modified, home-brewed creation, but they realized that it could not match the speed of the purpose-built machines that they were competing against. So the hybrid Fidderman/ Webster was replaced with a Derbyshire chassis, a purpose-built tubular spaceframe outfit designed to use car-type 13in diameter wheels and current low-profile racing tyres. The three-cylinder Suzuki engine was tuned and installed in this outfit, and the engine was placed much nearer the rear wheel than in the Fidderman, so contributing to much improved traction and handling.

The Derbyshire chassis is still being manufactured today, as the ASCO-Derbyshire, and is used by many clubmen in the F2 sidecar class, which allows 350cc two-stroke twins or 600cc four-stroke fours. Steve's Derbyshire was bought secondhand, but was a vast improvement on his previous outfit as it allowed the Webster brothers to run consistently at the front of the Auto 66 races, and indeed it was on the Derbyshire chassis that they recorded their first win. They won the Auto 66 Club Championship on the Derbyshire-Suzuki combination, but realized that the new four-cylinder Yamaha racing engines, in 500cc and 700cc forms, had much more power than their modified road engine.

Steve's next machine was a Windle short-chassis outfit powered by a full race specification Yamaha engine. The Terry Windle-built outfit was the best machine of its time, and again it was a tubular spaceframe kneeler. The Sheffield-based frame builder produced beautifully engineered machines which handled well. The four-cylinder Yamaha engine was essentially the same unit as used in the works 500cc Yamaha Grand Prix machines of the late 1970s, and ridden by the likes of Kenny Roberts and Giacomo Agostini. The engine had four cylinders in line, and employed conventional piston-port induction. This is where the piston opens a port, or hole, in the cylinder wall as it moves down the bore, so allowing the petrol/air mixture to be sucked into the engine. This type of two-stroke engine is relatively inefficient and 'dirty' due to the fact that a lot of unburnt fuel mixture is allowed to flow straight over the top of the piston on the induction stroke and straight out of the exhaust port before the piston rises and compresses the mixture and the spark ignites it. Tuning of this type of engine only increases the amount of unburnt fuel escaping to the atmosphere, because the traditional method of tuning two-strokes is to increase the size of the ports, so extending the time that they are open and allowing more fuel mixture to enter the cylinder. It is this unburnt fuel that creates the distinctive blue haze that follows many early two-stroke engines like their own personal smokescreen, and has led to environmentalists branding the two-stroke engine as a dirty pollutant. Webster used this type of engine until the 1987 season, when he changed over to the reed valve-inducted Krauser engine.

Although Steve had been delighted with his conventional short-chassis Windle outfit, he was less enamoured with the ex-Jock Taylor long-chassis Windle that Dennis Trollope provided for him. Terry Windle had correctly realized that the trend in Grand Prix racing was towards the longer chassis outfits that Rolf Biland had pioneered. The long-chassis 'worms' had better stability, traction, braking and cornering potential than the conventional short outfits. Windle's long-chassis outfit was a monocoque design. Perhaps it was the method of construction that led to the flexibility in the chassis that made it unstable and unpredictable. Steve never did get to grips with this machine. He admitted that it frightened him on several occasions, and eventually the outfit was badly damaged in the horrific accident that hospitalized Steve and Tony Hewitt on the Isle of Man. Webster never used the long-chassis Windle after that and never returned to the Island for the TT races.

Since 1986 Steve Webster has used a succession of LCR chassis manufactured in Switzerland by Louis Christian Racing. Although the LCR has been developed and refined over the years, the basic concept has not changed: the sleek all-enveloping glassfibre bodywork conceals a very sophisticated racing machine that has no peers in current sidecar Grands Prix. So good is the LCR that nearly every top-level competitor in the class uses the Swiss-built machine. Those that don't use very close copies of the trend-setting outfit.

The basis of the LCR is a very light but torsionally stiff aluminium monocoque that is bonded and riveted together. This monocoque comprises a long box, the front and rear ends of which curve away from the centre-line towards the wheels. The chassis has a short T-section box attached to it to form the sidecar outrigger, the front and rear of the main chassis tapers down to a smaller cross-section, and the aircraft-specification bag-type fuel tank is housed in the central section of the monocoque. The front suspension comprises two parallel wishbones manufactured from small-section welded steel tubes which carry the front hub and brake unit, and are bolted to the front of the monocoque. A pushrod from the bottom of the hub actuates the combined coil spring and damper unit, housed inside the front of the monocoque, via a bell crank and rocking lever to provide suspension movement. Steering is accomplished by conventional handlebars attached to a tube which curves around the wheel and attaches to the hub assembly. The throttle is a motorcycle-type twist grip on the right-hand bar, but the brake lever on this bar is not used, only being there to satisfy the requirements of the regulations. Instead, all braking is done by the left-foot-operated brake pedal. The gears are operated by the right foot. The clutch lever is on the left handlebar, a rev-counter and a water temperature gauge are provided, and there is an ignition cut-out device that attaches to the rider's wrist so that if he falls off the machine, the lead pulls out of its socket and cuts the motor.

The rear suspension has a lower wishbone which is suspended from the chassis at its wider end and is connected to the bottom of the cast aluminium upright at the other. The upper suspension component is a single tube, which is adjustable for length to provide camber adjustment. Fore-and-aft location is controlled by a tie-bar which runs from the top of the upright to the rear of the engine cradle and by a similar lower bar attached to the bottom of the upright, and to the gearbox supports at its forward end. The rear coil spring/damper unit is also mounted within the monocoque and is operated by a pushrod via bell cranks and rocking levers. The sidecar wheel is not fitted with suspension, but its twin wishbones and tie-rods are adjustable for camber, ride height and fore-and-aft adjustment. Both front and rear suspensions allow rapid adjustment of ride height, damper settings and spring rates. Additionally the rear toe-in can be adjusted by altering the length of the tie-rods.

The engine and separate gearbox are supported by a tubular steel cradle which is bolted to the aluminium moncoque just in front of the rear wheel. The drive to the rear wheel is by chain from the six-speed gearbox to a sprocket mounted on the rear upright. This sprocket can be changed to alter the overall gearing, and there is also a choice of gearbox ratios to provide optimum intermediate gearing.

All three wheels are fitted with disc brakes. The front and rear on Steve's bike are made of carbon-fibre; the sidecar brake disc is a conventional iron disc. All three discs are 240mm in diameter and use four-piston calipers manufactured by AP Racing, of Leamington Spa. The braking system employs two master-cylinders, one for the front wheel, the other operating the rear and sidecar wheels. The split or percentage of total braking force applied by each master-cylinder can be adjusted. This is a necessity because the rider requires more braking effort to be applied to the rear wheel in wet conditions, when the front could lock up and cause loss of control. In the dry, the majority of the braking effort is directed to the front brake. At the time of writing, Webster had been the only rider to use carbon-fibre brakes so far; however, several other competitors were expected to be using them during 1992.

Apart from their well-known ability to resist fading over a long race distance, the carbon discs are also lighter and smaller than cast iron units. Biland needs to use 290mm cast-iron units to achieve similar results to Steve's 240mm carbon discs, and at the end of a long hot race the cast-iron brakes will be far less effective than their carbon counterparts. The disadvantages of carbon discs are that they take longer to warm up to operating temperature, and in the rain it is often necessary to apply gentle pressure on the brake pedal on the straights to bring the discs up to temperature. Steve feels that the widespread adoption of carbon-fibre brakes will lead to accidents, as some of the less experienced competitors will forget to bring their brakes up to temperature in the frantic action of the early laps. The carbon rotors are also extremely fragile as they will fracture at the slightest impact, so great care has to be taken by the spanner men to prevent an accidental tap on the carbon disc, which could destroy it.

The radiator for the water-cooled engine is mounted in front of the sidecar outrigger chassis extension, and the water pipes that carry the coolant are routed through the chassis to the cylinders. The sidecar bodywork has a large opening in front of the chair to direct cool air through the radiator. Steve uses an oil cooler, mounted on the rear of the main chassis, to cool the gearbox oil and the air inlet for this cooler can be blanked off in cool weather.

The passenger's perch is a small area of carbon-fibre floor riveted and bonded, using Araldite, to the rear and outrigger chassis box sections. The passenger has several grab handles positioned on the chair and on the bike's bodywork, the main one being a vertical handle on the chair which is the main anchor point for his left hand.

The Webster LCR rides on Ronal 13in diameter wheels shod with Avon tyres; the front wheel is usually 8.2in wide although different widths can be used for certain types of circuit. The sidecar wheel is normally 9in wide, and at the rear a 10in rim width is usually employed, but Steve has experimented with a 14in diameter by 10in wide wheel on the rear.

The motive power for this piece of high technology craftsmanship is a four-cylinder two-stroke engine of 498cc capacity producing in excess of 150bhp. For the 1992 season, Steve has switched from the ubiquitous Krauser engine to the ADM, as used by Rolf Biland in 1991. The two engines are in fact very similar, as would be expected with both of them being manufactured by the same person. The reason for the switch to the ADM is that it uses a more recent design of cylinder. The bottom end of the engine is based on the old inline four-cylinder Yamaha unit and uses the built-up and pressed together Yamaha crankshafts. The crankcases have been extensively modified to allow reed valve-controlled crankcase induction to be used. This means that instead of the fuel-air mixture being sucked into the cylinder, it is drawn into the bottom of the crankcase through the reed valves, which only open when the piston is creating suction by travelling up the bore, and is then pushed into the top of the cylinder through transfer ports which run up the side of the cylinder wall. The transfer ports are cut into the cylinder at a level which puts them above the exhaust ports, so preventing the loss of unburnt fuel which made the piston port inducted two-stroke so inefficient. This layout produces far more power than the older design and allows much more accurate port timing and control of the combustion process, leading to greater efficiency and more power over a wider rev range.

A critical part of this engine is the use of Honda 125cc cylinders as used by the 125cc solo racers. These cylinders are coated with Nikasil which is a very hard surface coating, allowing very close piston-to-cylinder tolerances and being less affected by temperature distortion at high revs than uncoated cylinders. In effect the ADM and Krauser engines are four separate cylinders mounted on a common crankcase. Each cylinder has a 38mm Mikuni flat-slide carburettor to provide the fuel-air mixture. A large collector box houses the carburettors to ensure a consistent intake pressure, and to prevent foreign objects such as stones and dirt entering the fragile engine.

The exhaust system is actually an integral part of the engine, as the shape and capacity of the exhaust expansion chambers dictate the amount of back-pressure which helps to close the exhaust port and raise the compression ratio in the cylinders. A skilled tuner can alter the power characteristics of a two-stroke engine by changing the shape of the exhaust system. It can be used to provide power at low revs by reducing the volume in the expansion chambers, or top-end power can be gained, at the expense of a narrower power band, by increasing the pulse rate of the exhaust gases. The exhausts on the LCR run forwards before turning through 90 degrees and exiting via a collector box just behind the front wheel. However, such a description provides only an outline regarding this vital part of the engine. The whole subject of two-stroke exhaust systems is highly complex, and very much a black art, requiring greater technical explanation than this book is intended to cover.

Away from the technical complexities of these three-wheeled racing machines, areas such as the quality of driver handling and the importance of the contribution of the passenger to a fast lap of a Grand Prix circuit must now be considered.

A racing sidecar outfit is a bit of an oddball: it is neither bike nor car and its handling is as strange as its looks! For a start the machine handles differently on right and left-hand bends; its assymetric layout and unequal weight distribution means that the driver has to adopt a different approach in getting the machine to turn left or right. On left-hand bends Steve can use the power to make the back end drift and tighten the line through the corner. In car racing terms this could be the equivalent of power-induced oversteer. He has to be careful, though, because with the passenger's weight hung outside the sidecar wheel, the lightly loaded rear driving wheel can spin and cause the outfit to lose traction. If it then suddenly grips, it is possible for the sidecar wheel to raise into the air, and – in extreme circumstances – tip the whole outfit over. On right-hand bends the passenger's weight is placed over the driven wheel, so that excessive power can still spin the rear wheel and cause the outfit to drift, but it is just as likely for the front end to plough straight on in the classic understeering pose. To drive one of these outfits quickly requires years of practice and an understanding and co-ordination of effort between driver and passenger that defies belief.

The role of the passenger is to provide an adjustment to the weight distribution to enable the driver to put as much power to the road surface as possible, and to achieve the maximum speed through corners without detracting from the outfit's straight-line capabilities. There are three basic positions for the passenger and numerous subtle little variations on these positions which the top passengers refine into race-winning performances. When the machine is travelling in a straight line, the passenger will curl himself up behind the sidecar fairing out of the airstream to reduce wind resistance and aid top speed. Through a left-handed corner, the passenger leans out of the outfit behind the sidecar wheel with his bottom rubbing along the track surface, hence the use of knee sliders on the passenger's bottom. On right-hand turns, the sidecar passenger puts his body over the rear wheel fairing, with his head nearly brushing the track surface. This position also aids traction out of slow corners by putting extra weight over the driven wheel, thus preventing wheelspin.

A better idea of how the driver and passenger have to interact together may be achieved by describing a lap of Steve's favourite circuit, Donington Park, and examining Gavin Simmon's contribution to it.

On a flying lap, Steve is accelerating hard over the start and finish line in fourth gear, changing up into fifth and then sixth, before the right-hand Redgate Corner. Gavin, meanwhile, is tucked down behind the fairing, unable to see the road. He waits until he can feel Steve braking before he sits up and climbs over the rear wheel. Steve brakes hard and changes down to third gear, gradually feeding in the power as the machine is turned right. Then he has to make two or three small steering corrections as the machine fights for grip.

Gavin stays over the driving wheel until the corner starts to straighten out, but he needs to keep the majority of his weight over the rear wheel as Steve accelerates through fourth and fifth gears because they are still sweeping right through Holywood. Steve gets top gear on the exit of the right-hander and swoops flat-out down the hill to the left-hand kink called Craner Curves. This is a very difficult and important section for Gavin; out of Holywood he has to move from over the rear wheel, to lean out to the left of the chair for Craner Curves, and then get back over the rear wheel for the very fast right-hand bend called the Old Hairpin. These movements across the machine have to be effected smoothly as a sudden violent movement would throw the machine off line at 130mph and would probably result in a sizeable accident.

Steve takes the Old Hairpin in fourth gear, changing up into fifth as the sidecar wheel vibrates on the rumble strips on the corner's exit kerbing. As Steve accelerates through the gearbox, Gavin again has to move from over the rear wheel to the left of the chair as the machine climbs the hill up to McLeans. The long sweeping left-hand climb requires a delicate balancing act from Gavin: his bottom brushes the grass on the left-hand approach to McLeans and he has to position his body quickly over the rear wheel as Steve brakes very hard and changes down to third for the right-hand corner.

McLeans is taken flat-out in third, with the outfit drifting out onto the rumble strips. Gavin eases himself off the rear wheel when the machine is straight and briefly ducks down behind the cowling as the outfit climbs the short hill to the long sweeping right-hander at Coppice. This is a very difficult and important corner for both men. Steve has to balance the machine's desire to understeer on the way in, whilst Gavin has to get his weight over the driven wheel to stop it spinning too much and losing traction on the way out. Coppice corner leads onto the longest and fastest straight on the circuit, so it is important to carry good speed

Friends and rivals Webster/Simmons, Michel/Birchall, Streuer/de Haas and Biland/Waltisperg battling for the early lead in the 1990 Yugoslavian GP at Rijeka, where Webster and Simmons were to finish third. (*David Goldman*)

A Bit on the Side! Gavin Simmons, 'bumming' around in the Spanish dust on their way to victory in the 1991 GP, demonstrates the fine balance needed to complement Webster's racing line. (*David Goldman*)

The LCR chassis without its distinctive glassfibre bodywork clearly showing the rearward mounting of the Krauser engine with its complex exhaust system and massive cold air box for the carburettors. (*David Goldman*)

Smiles from Webster and Simmons in the pit lane prior to the 1990 British GP at Donington would soon turn sour after a poor start from pole position. A heavy collision quickly followed, forcing their retirement on the first lap. (*David Goldman*)

Following the shock announcement of the collapse of his sponsor, Brown Brothers, Webster ran with advertising space available on the fairing of his outfit as he struggled to find replacement funds. (*David Goldman*)

Fortunately, BSB Satellite TV stepped into the breach to rescue Steve's 1990 season. (*David Goldman*)

Steve Webster MBE at Buckingham Palace for the investiture in 1990. Sidecar racing does have its rewards! (*Kenneth Bray*)

Webster and Hewitt lead a packed sidecar field into Redgate Corner at Donington. 'Get Redgate right,' says Steve, 'and it's the key to a fast lap.' (*John Colley*)

Webster and Simmons racing in the 1991 Czech GP against the background of a deserted Brno circuit. Steve took no risks with a temperamental gearbox and settled for third place. (*David Goldman*)

Webster the family man. Steve with Karen, their baby daughter Holly and infant son Simon. (*Mick Webster*)

'Not the Brazilian GP' at Le Mans in 1991. Steve and Gavin finished in third place, which was sufficient to secure Simmons' first and Webster's fourth World Championship. (*David Goldman*)

A World Champion's machinery laid bare in the pit lane at Magny Cours in 1992. (*Henk Keulemans*)

All that stood between Steve Webster and his fifth World Championship in 1992. Rolf Biland and Kurt Waltisperg getting down to business at Magny Cours. (*Henk Keulemans*)

Teamwork 1. Webster and Simmons perform their famous balancing act at Magny Cours in 1992. (*Henk Keulemans*)

Teamwork 2. Steve Webster at the Royal Automobile Club, in London, after being presented with the Segrave Trophy by the Ford Motor Company Chairman Ian MacAllister. With him are Mick Webster, Mary Smith and Gavin Simmons, all of whom received Segrave Medals for their part in his success. (*Ford Motor Company*)

through the corner and to get good drive out of it, as this will determine the outfit's maximum speed at the end of the straight.

Gavin has to stay over the rear wheel just long enough to provide the maximum traction out of the corner because if he gets down behind the fairing too soon the machine will lose grip and be slow onto the straight. If he stays over the rear wheel for too long, he will act as an air brake and cost the machine valuable speed at the end of the straight. At this point in the lap Simmons gets his only chance to rest. He is tucked in behind the fairing for all of six or seven seconds before he has to tackle the Esses, a vicious left followed immediately by an equally tight right. This corner is approached in sixth gear at 150mph and requires very heavy use of the carbon fibre brakes, and Steve has to change down into second gear. Gavin, meanwhile, is performing his acrobatics again, sat up in the chair to aid braking stability. He has to get out behind the sidecar wheel for the first element, then quickly over to the right and over the outfit's rear wheel for the right-hander, and then back under the fairing for the blast down to the Melbourne Hairpin. No-one really likes this part of the Donington circuit; the Grand Prix loop was only added to the original circuit in order to bring it up to the required distance for a Grand Prix track. It comprises the Esses and two first-gear corners linked by two straights, thus calling for three heavy brake applications and two flat-out sprints, so that it doesn't tax the skill of any rider or driver. The Melbourne Hairpin is a right-hander and is approached downhill. The climb out of this turn leads to the left-hand Goddards Corner, which falls away on the exit. Goddards is a difficult corner for a sidecar passenger, because, being a left-hand bend, it requires Gavin to be leaning out of the chair; but the exit of the corner, on to the start and finish straight, needs him to get over to the other side of the machine to aid traction out of the slow corner. All that remains of the lap is about 100 yards of flat-out acceleration to the finishing line. If Steve and Gavin have worked well together, the 2½-miles lap of Donington will have been covered in just under 98 seconds at an average speed of 92mph or 148km/h!

To be a top-class sidecar passenger requires strength, fitness and athleticism in large quantities. Mick Webster reckons that you have to be barking mad as well!

10
Friends and Rivals

'There is no doubt about it,' remarks Steve, 'when you ask me about friends and rivals, the overriding thought that comes to mind is that racing can be a very cruel sport. It's exciting and glamorous; it's demanding and rewarding; but there are times when the ultimate price is paid for the thrill of the moment.'

One of Steve's closest friends was injured cruelly by the sport in 1987, and naturally he found it very hard to talk about Derek Bayley without a great deal of emotion.

'Here is a man whom I've a mountain of respect for. He was always trying to help me, very often at his own expense. He'd spend time advising me and then I'd go and beat him, and he was always delighted for me – never ever bitter or disappointed that he hadn't won. He'd always got time for people and had such a sunny disposition. We'd worked closely together with the Krauser engine and our enthusiasm had sparked each other off. I was looking forward to him coming over to Austria for the Grand Prix in 1987. We'd gone straight to Austria, but Derek had stopped off in the Isle of Man for the TT races. Derek had actually been taking a break from racing and had only recently come back into it. The first we knew that anything was wrong was when someone in the paddock had phoned home and had been told that Derek had experienced a bad crash in practice. On making further enquiries I was saddened to hear that poor Derek wasn't expected to recover and the term "only a matter of time", was applied to his situation.

'As soon as I got home I went to Walton Hospital, in Liverpool, to see Derek, and I felt physically sick at what I saw. The feeling of helplessness just sweeps over you. All the times that Derek had gone out of his way to help me, and now here he was on a life support machine and there wasn't a single thing I could do to help him. He looked dreadful, his head was terribly swollen. Is this what a sport can do to you? I went to the hospital on several occasions and although I didn't know if Derek could hear me or not I chatted away to him for hours about racing and what was going on.'

Eventually, Derek did recover a little, was allowed home and is seen occasionally around racing paddocks. He cannot speak and his co-ordination is affected, but Steve still talks to him as if he was the Derek of old.

'Coping with a disabled person often makes people feel awkward, but I refuse to accept that Derek doesn't know what is going on, even though he can't speak. I was convinced of this at Donington, when I was explaining to him about the cylinders that I was trying. I told him that I was comparing the Yamahas with the Hummel cylinders. Derek listened and then picked up the cylinders and looked down the bore and nodded in agreement. Just for a minute the old Derek was sitting there in our transporter, it really gets to me. Yes, racing is a cruel sport.'

This statement was underlined in October of 1991 when Steve lost a close friend at Brands Hatch. 'This is my recurring nightmare,' says Steve. 'The moment I've always dreaded happened to me on that sunny Saturday morning. I wake up in the middle of the night now and think that Graham will be all right in a minute and he'll come running down the track to get back on the bike.'

Steve had contacted Graham Rose in early October to do a round of the Shell series at Brands Hatch on October 19. Gavin was unavailable because he was going to the Congress in Brazil to collect his World Championship medal. This was Gavin's first World Championship award, and Steve's fourth, so Steve felt that the moment was to be more special for Gavin and his family and that Gavin must go to the Congress. Gavin had been a bit undecided as this trip meant missing Brands Hatch, which was a meeting where potential sponsors and their guests would be present, and he'd also miss the Day of Champions, a fund-raising day for the Save the Children charity at Donington. However, Webster was insistent: 'I could remember how much fun Tony and

I had when we went to get our first medals in France. It was one of those unforgettable experiences and I was determined. Gav deserved it.'

So, off Simmons went and left Steve to find a replacement passenger for the Brands Hatch round and Donington. The appearance at Brands was to attempt to interest Readymix Concrete in a sponsorship deal. 'I thought about ringing Julian Tailford, says Steve, who passengers for my brother Kevin, and I also considered a local lad called Tony Atkinson. Then I got talking to Barry Brindley, and Graham's name came up. I hadn't thought of him initially as I'd heard he'd retired. I had known Graham for many years, he was around on the clubbie circuit in 1983 with a lad called Stiratt, and he'd worked with Barry Brindley from 1985 to 1987. He was well-respected as a good passenger. I rang him up but he was away on holiday, so I left a message on his answering machine. If only you could turn the clock back ... When he wasn't there, why didn't I ring someone else? The times I go over this situation are infinite. Graham responded to my message and said he'd be delighted to passenger me. He'd worked with Barry recently in America and was eager to get back into racing. He also said he'd just split up with his girlfriend and so he needed cheering up and a blast round a circuit was just the ticket. He was really enthusiastic.

'He came up to stay the night before the race and we went out for a pint together. It's ridiculous to say it now, but I got to know Graham better that evening than I had in all the eight years I'd known him. We discussed all sorts of things: his relationship with his girlfriend that had just ended; what we thought about sponsorship; how we manged our finances. We talked well into the night. My dad and Mary had taken the bike to Brands and so we had a fairly leisurely drive down there in my car, still nattering away and generally putting the world to rights. We seemed to have found a closeness that we'd never shared before. We talked about the private sides of our personalities in a way that blokes rarely do.'

The practice at Brands got off to a good start: 'It felt just like Tony had got back on the bike. Graham's weight and his riding style are very similar to Tony's. Gavin is lighter and has a different approach whereas Graham was like Tony in that he was smooth and he always did just enough to stay on the pace, and kept a little in reserve. He felt totally in time with me. The weather was perfect, our spirits were high. Between us we were determined that we would win. We did five laps and pulled into the pits, Dad checked the tyres and we went out for another five laps. When we pulled in this time we both complained that our arms were aching. Brands is a bumpy track so I changed my gloves and after the usual pit lane checks we set off again. As I left the hairpin I felt the bike go light on the front wheel and I thought, "Oh heck, we've lost it!" I struggled to straighten the outfit and pulled on to the grass to give Graham a chance to run and jump back on. When he didn't come immediately, I started to look around and I saw the marshals motioning to the safety crew. So I ran back up the track. All credit due to the Brands Hatch marshals and safety team, they were there within seconds. By the time I reached the scene, the doctor was already there. I just couldn't believe it – this was not a particularly fast part of the circuit, and not a place where you'd worry about a serious accident. The doctor was struggling with Graham's helmet and he asked me to release the strap. I did this, looked at Graham – and I just knew. Deep down inside I knew, and yet I refused to believe that Graham was dead. The doctor was listening to Graham's chest and doing various checks but he never took his eyes off me. I realized that if there was any hope at all, the doctor would not be focusing his attention on me. Time stood absolutely still. A rescue vehicle took me to the well-equipped hospital that is on the circuit. The facilities at Brands are second to none, many a life has been saved because of the services on hand there. They have vital equipment for stabilizing injured people, so maybe I was wrong. Perhaps in a minute they'd sort Graham out. I looked up when one of the doctors came into the room: "I'm sorry Steve", was all he said. I felt stunned. One moment we were powering around the picturesque Kent circuit, full of high hopes for a victory; the next, here I was listening to a doctor going through formalities. All the things Graham had said to me last night, all those hopes and feelings, all were irrelevant now.

'I was beset with guilt, and I still am. I know that there was nothing that I was doing on the bike that caused Graham to fall off. It's just the question of, if I'd not rung him, if we'd not done that particular lap … and so it goes on. Spectators who saw the accident tell me that Graham just lost his grip, he slid very slowly from the bike but must have broken his neck when he hit the tyre wall. To the onlookers it didn't look like a fatality and they too expected him to be winded, but nothing more serious. It was one of those freak accidents, but it will stay with me forever. All I can console myself with is that when Graham was on the bike he was enjoying himself, he was riding with someone he had always wanted to ride with and his heart was set on a rostrum place. Bike racing is a glamorous sport, but here in a split second and without warning the ultimate price was paid.'

Steve fears that in years to come he will get slower and slower as he feels so aware of his own mortality. 'When I think back to some of my racing manoeuvres, I shudder. Racing is a calculated risk. You don't think twice about the dangers when you are young and crazy, but as you get older the more dangerous it becomes. Once I feel my concentration is going and I start to wonder what the kids are doing at home when I'm halfway round a corner, that's when I'll call it a day.'

'I can remember coming into the paddock in France in tears because I'd seen the aftermath of an accident and thought that Simon Birchall had been killed. As I went past there was a mass of machinery and bodies and I saw Simon's outfit. All I could think was that Simon's girlfriend, Sandra, was in the pit lane and how could I tell her? As it turned out Simon had stopped to help a German rider who was fatally injured. I felt awful for being so relieved. That poor rider was someone else's Simon. These things don't happen very often, thankfully, but they are memories that stay with you forever.'

In car racing, sports psychologists are commonplace, but riders also need coping strategies to combat the dangers of the job. Steve finds talking about his feelings a great leveller, whereas Simon, who has seen more than his fair share of serious injury, blocks it out. 'Simon saved the life of a team member by his fast action and basic knowledge of first aid,' recalls Steve; 'he applied a tourniquet to a severed limb; he is very good in a crisis.'

It turns out that Simon is a very interesting character all round! His stripping activities in Austria have already been related, but it seems Simon is larger than life in more than one sense of the word! 'Simon Birchall and Alain Michel teamed up in 1990,' recalls Steve, 'at the same time as Gavin and myself. Gavin and I gelled straight away, but Simon and Alain had a more rocky road to success.

'Both Alain and Simon are extremes in their own right. They had to learn to compromise and to cope with each other's strong personalities. Alain had always had French passengers before and I'm sure he won't mind me saying that he did tend to treat them as subservient. No-one had ever contradicted him or answered him back before. Michel does not trust people, he likes to be at the helm of any activity in the team and so inevitably the book stops with him. To be told, "Forget it, sirrah, tha's a prat", was not the kind of post-race analysis that he was used to! He also thought that his Yorkshire counterpart had some very funny habits. Alain would say to me: "I cannot understand it, Steve. He goes for a walk around the track, and he is gone for hours. When he comes back, he is pissed!" What Michel didn't appreciate is that the English way of using one's leisure time is not quite the same as the French way. I tried to tell Alain that whereas he enjoyed a bottle of vintage wine with his meal and would sit and chat over the Armagnac, Simon was more of the "several pints and good sing song" brigade! On the occasion where he had disappeared to inspect the track and come back the worse for wear, I was in fact with him. We had discovered a bar in the paddock, and various riders were there and it had turned into a bit of a party. The thing with Simon is that he would never drink before race day, and he would certainly never let Alain down on the bike. I tried to tell Alain this as best I could!

'Alain would get totally exasperated with Simon and he would be shaking with rage. One memorable occasion was the 'plug chop' at Spa. A 'plug chop' is carried out by all two-stroke racers. It is done at the end of a practice session to determine whether or not the carburation has been set correctly. The procedure is to get the machine to maximum speed and engine revolutions, and then cut the ignition, simultaneously pulling in the clutch. This ensures that when the sparking plugs are removed they show the mixture strength at maximum engine revs under load. A weak mixture could mean premature detonation and seizure, whereas too rich, and the engine will not be producing its maximum horsepower. This may cause the plugs to foul and the engine to misfire at high revs. Correct carburation is the keynote to success in any two-stroke racing engine, but many people still believe it to be a black art and secrets are carefully guarded. However, the 'plug chop' is still the most accurate indicator of whether or not the carburation is correct. The arrangement at Spa was for all the outfits to do their 'plug chop' on the last lap of practice and then to be directed to the pits the 'wrong' way around the circuit. The pairs were lined up to coast back to the pits when two warring figures could be seen on the horizon: "Mon Dieu, c'est impossible!", came the cry, followed by "Ah, and if tha thinks I'm getting on there, when you f***ing ride like that, you've another think coming". They really were just about coming to blows.

'The 1990 season was punctuated with French expletives and Yorkshire growls – most entertaining! Dad and I put them together and helped them all we could, and then they beat us!' Steve tries to iron out the cultural differences between these two whenever he can: 'Then they agree that they are the best of pals, but when they disagree … good lord,' he sighs. It is a fact that the racing paddocks of Europe will be a quieter and less colourful place without this pair, as Alain Michel has announced his retirement. He will be much missed.

It is hard to describe the relationship between rider and passenger as they have to trust each other with their lives. 'I have been very fortunate,' remarks Steve, 'with both Tony and Gavin. Tony refined my style and protected me from myself. I was too wild and he calmed me down and polished up my act. For Gavin, this was a hard act to follow but he has done the role justice because he is a perfectionist. He aims to win and to this end trains vigorously, hiding his gritty determination beneath a quiet, shy exterior. Every move he makes on the bike is well planned and carried out with great skill and talent. From the word "Go", we worked well together.'

Just as Michel and Birchall found it hard to gell as a pair, Abbot and Smith are a pair who are inseparable. 'If they are apart in the paddock,' laughs Steve, 'you can bet your life they are looking for each other. Their friendship has stood the test of time and the pressures of racing. They get on well on the track and they socialize a lot together, too.' Steve's relationship with Steve Abbott and Shaun Smith goes back a long way as they have been there ever since the famous Carnaby days. Steve recognizes that they haven't had the breaks that he's had, but he is in no doubt that the talent is there. On the plus side, they probably haven't upset as many people. Everybody has a soft spot for them. Steve Abbott is a renowned prankster, a bundle of fun, looking for somewhere to explode. He is also legendary for his stringent winter testing programme – walking the dog and going to the pub!

Like Webster, Steve Abbot had also had a brief period sponsored by the Padgett concern. 'Shaun and Steve left the Padgetts without as much fuss as I caused,' said Steve; 'they would accept it if things went wrong, whereas I never do.' But Steve Abbott is a hard racer who will not give in on the track. If there is a dispute going into a corner, you can bet your life Steve will come out first. 'He's a determined rider,' comments Steve, 'and he won't give in!' Webster describes Steve Abbott as a very thorough race engineer with a real eye for chassis development. 'He isn't afraid to alter chassis design completely,' remarks Webster, 'he is a wizard with suspension. Given the right equipment and a few lucky breaks, Abbott and Smith could go far.'

One rival who has had the breaks and certainly has the equipment is Rolf Biland. He is the one rival that Steve has mentioned time and time again. 'He was one of my heroes from a very early age,' states Steve 'and I hold him in the highest esteem. In fact I used to put him on a bit of a pedestal. Rolf is very good at finding the finance to make sure his outfit is in tip-top form. If half the money is there, Biland can find the other half. He likes to be different, and this flair for the unusual attracts the sponsors. If ever there is a V4 in sidecar GP racing Rolf will have it. His strikingly shaped bodywork was a real eyecatcher, and this draws sponsors in. Until recently, I was psychologically fazed by the tales of Biland the great engineer. I now find out that this is a myth and that in fact Rolf is not mechanically minded. His success is that he surrounds himself with excellent mechanics and engine tuners. I have also discovered that another chink in his armour is that he is quick to act on people's suggestions even if they are not really sure of the advice they are giving! Honestly, if the postman came in and commented on the tuning, Rolf would alter it. I know he calls me Mr Standard, but there are times when his individuality has cost him the World Championship.

'Sometimes Rolf has done some really strange things. For instance, in Mugello, he was trying out two sets of carburation: one arrangement that would get him off the line like a rocket, but be down on power out on the circuit; and an alternative that was slow off the line, but powerful in the race. Oddly, he chose to run the fast-starting one, and consequently he had to pull in after a few laps. Surely, a rider of Biland's calibre does not really have to worry about a lightning start. With his talent it would only take a few laps to claw his way to the forefront of the action anyway.

Undoubtedly, Rolf's specialist subject is aerodynamics. He is a master at creating fairings, but again he was caught out by his unusual fairing in the 1991 season when he discovered in testing at Mouton that his outfit had 15kg of downforce, whereas the Webster machine had only 3kg; this was slowing Biland down. So after work in a wind-tunnel following Assen Biland was sorted out and he flew!

'But you have to feel sorry for Biland, sometimes; he was really keen to get the points system altered, so that our two poorest scores were dropped. This worked against him and helped me to win the Championship!'

Biland is not used to people pulling his leg or laughing at his misfortunes. Most people hold his magnanimous talent in such high regard that they hardly dare even speak to him. However, Derek Jones, 'Crazy horse', would have to be the exception. 'I put his confidence with Rolf down to him spending a considerable amount of his racing career upside down,' laughs Steve; 'there aren't many riders who have actually deposited their passengers up trees, but Derek has always liked to be different! Like Biland, really, but Derek went a different way about it. It was Derek who dared to snigger as he saw Rolf go off at the chicane at Le Mans. Rolf lost control coming out of the chicane, but he did exactly the right thing: he threw the bike across the gravel and into the sand; his passenger fell out and Biland was relieved that no-one had seen this little error. He was not aware of the demonic Derek high up in the grandstand. Derek could not get into the paddock quickly enough to run his finger over the rear wheel, discover specks of sand and say, "Tut tut, Rolf – been on the beach again!" Rolf was not amused! No-one would dare do this but Derek!

'There are those who feel that racing should be all rivalry and very little friendship. We are rivals on the track. Rolf and I are definitely rivals, but we understand each other. In Sweden, in 1988, Rolf did try to push me off the track. He wanted to win and he is capable of desperate measures. We both know where we stand. I don't blame him for wanting to win, but I'm not fazed by him. I know what makes him tick!

'I know in Mugello in 1991 he wanted the Egloffs to help him to stop me scoring points. I dropped back as I didn't want to be driven off the track. Gav was going mad and hammering on my helmet, but Biland was four laps down on us, and I'd got it in hand. It was a time when I wished we'd got helmet-to-helmet intercoms. It's psychological warfare with Rolf, but I'm a fair match, I hope!'

Although Biland is impressive, the man that Steve refers to as the Professor is Egbert Streuer. 'Egbert has been World Champion three times, in 1984, 1985 and 1986, and I'm sure he'd have been it again if he hadn't been dogged by passenger problems,' comments Steve. 'Schneiders and Streuer were a very good pair. But it is my opinion that Schneiders became complacent. He stopped winter training and imagined that he could jump back on the bike and be competitive in the spring. This, of course, sadly, isn't the case. Throughout the winter most riders have a strict regime of going to the gym, motocrossing and playing perhaps squash or some other physically demanding game that will build up their stamina. Schneiders tried to miss out the winter regime and his performance suffered.

'When it comes to engines, however, Streuer is very knowledge-able, clever both with technology and engine development.' As Steve says, it is finding the right passenger that has been Egbert's downfall. He rode for a while with Gerald de Haas but they fell out over the financial arrangements and the division of labour in the team. One of Egbert's most unusual passengers is Harry, yes – just Harry. Harry is a lad from behind the bar, back in Holland, whom Egbert took on one night whilst on an alcoholic high.

'I was delighted when Peter Brown and Egbert got together,' says Webster. 'Peter is very, very good. Streuer is a positive rider as he goes into corners tightly, brakes hard and pulls out fast. Peter complements it beautifully. They are a good pairing and one to watch in '92 and beyond.'

Someone else to watch out for, in Steve's opinion, is Barry Brindley. 'Barry's riding style just gets better and better. If World Championships were won on pure effort, Barry would have won times over. His biggest problem is, he's too nice. He's a real gentleman in all his dealings, but on the track he will back off and it gives others the opportunity to nip through. He tries to be a hard racer, but it just isn't in his nature. I'd love to be on the rostrum with him. I do hope his rostrum position isn't too far away. I know he will do it, it's just a matter of time. Barry is slowly progressing. He is absolutely marvellous in the wet and second only to Streuer, I would say. He is just as out of control as the rest of us in the wet, but he seems to cope with it. He isn't over-aggressive and he doesn't over-correct. He can beat me in the wet. But one thing that Barry must remedy is that it takes him two laps to get his racing head on, and in a race you don't have two laps to spare.'

What of younger brother Derek Brindley? 'Ah, Derek,' muses Steve, 'yes, he's quick, he's a real thinker, but he's still got a lot to learn. A star of the future without a doubt.

'The pair I really tip for the top are Ralf Bonhorst and Klaus Klaffenboch. They are still young hotshoes at the minute, but they've a lot of potential. They tend to get over-excited, but then again I can remember someone else who was like that once. They could well be future World Champions.'

On the subject of the British pair Fisher and Crone, Steve believes that they have found it hard to make the transition from four-stroke to two-stroke: 'It's getting the breaks that counts and 110 per cent dedication!'

Steve watches the progress of one prospect very carefully, and that is the attempts in the National rounds of brother Kevin. The last time we saw Kevin he was being loaded into an ambulance with a badly broken leg. Had events been different, Webster and Webster may well have been a household name. However, Kevin's career was not entirely halted by his spill at Elvington, but it certainly delayed his progress. He returned seriously to Club racing in 1985 as a passenger for York rider Mick Smith, who was racing a Triumph outfit.

After a spell as a passenger Kevin decided that he wanted to ride, so Steve stepped in to help. 'If determination and enthusiasm were anything to do with it Kevin would definitely be a World

Champion,' says Steve. He bought Steve's old chassis and Steve supplied an engine. Kevin teamed-up with Julian Tailford and the pair worked well in contesting the Shell Superbike and *MCN* rounds.

'Going to watch Kev is a real test of my nerves,' Steve admits. 'When I started racing, my mum used to say to me: "Don't go too fast!" and I'd chirp "fast enough". It became a bit of a family cliche. Now I find myself saying that to Kev – only more strongly. I went to watch him at Cadwell in September 1991 and he was far too fast. I think Dad and I being there had made him all hyped up, but once he settled down he was smoother and therefore quicker, even though he perhaps wasn't trying as hard. His passenger is a real broad Geordie, whatever you ask him you get a non-committal "Aye", except for once when Kev asked, "Is there anywhere I can go faster?" "Aye", came the response. "Well, where?" probed Kevin. "Everywhere!" came the experienced answer. I recognize the rush Kevin is in to do well. I worry about his safety. I have helped him by supplying engines but I sometimes wonder if I should help him. I don't want to be responsible for any accidents, but he'd race anyway, just as I would, but I do worry!'

The pairing of two brothers Webster and Webster never did make the world stage, but there are plenty of brothers who have. Perhaps the most well-known British pair are the Dixons.

Darren and Sean Dixon are from Folkestone in Kent. Darren is a hard worker, and the brother who does all the sponsor hunting, but I think Sean and he often have their differences. Darren is a good all-round sportsman, he is a leading goal scorer in the Avon Tyres football team and renowned for staying on the 'Bucking Bronco' at Brands Hatch when it spat out an entire World Championship side. He is as competent with a motocross bike as he is with a solo. Darren likes to live life to the full, much to the amazement of the foreign lads who are devoted to preparation and regard the English as inscrutible 'party animals'.

Darren started on the Club circuit in 1981 partnering Terry McGahan. He was really thrown in at the deep end on a Grand Prix Windle Yamaha. At first Darren didn't think he would get on with sidecars at all; the pain in his wrists from wrestling the beast was so intense that after his inaugural outing he was ready to wave – if he could have waved – goodbye to the chairs forever. He had retired in agony after only two laps at Lydden. Nevertheless he stuck at it and soon he and Terry were regular winners, especially at their local Kent circuits. In the sidecar club races of the early 1980s, Dixon and McGahan would regularly beat Webster. In 1982, Darren and Terry led the Clubmans Championship, and it has already been described how the Webster team pipped them at the post by their polythene sheeting tweek in a rain-lashed final. After this Darren disappeared from the sidecar show for a while and took the solo route – a move that didn't actually do him any harm – and he won the prestigious British title in 1985. Darren thought it was the end of the road when the consistent Club racers Webster and Webster beat him and McGahan in 1982, but a friend let him have a spirit-raising blast on an ex-Gary Lingham RG500 Mk 6. Darren was lightningly quick and this ride led to a season of spectacular wins and even more spectacular crashes. Living on the breadline and heavily supported by family and friends, Darren ended up third to Donnie Mcleod and Niall Mackenzie in the 1986 British 250 Championship. This same year Steve and Tony won their first Grand Prix. Darren fell out with his sponsors, Padgetts of Batley, and swapped to Francis Neill's team. He ended up fifth in the Euroatlantic series, but he couldn't cope with the RC30 and he didn't ride in the British Grand Prix. Darren then just packed it in and in order to ride in Grands Prix at a level he could afford, returned to sidecars. He patched up relations with the now famous Padgetts and they let Darren and brother Shaun loose on three wheels at Mallory. They were so amazed by the prowess of the brothers that they sponsored them for the Euro series in 1990 and for Grands Prix in 1991. 'I think 1992 is the year we will see great things from Darren,' predicted Webster, 'I knew way back in those clubbie days that Darren had the ability to make it to the top.'

Another family pairing is the Guedels, ex-karters: 'Never follow them; they are so precise that you have no margin for error,' Steve advises. 'They are close to the edge all the time, and to follow them unnerves me. I once tried to follow them in practice and I nearly crashed. They are very talented!'

Also very talented, but sadly no longer racing, are the Zurbrugg brothers. Martin and Alfred Zurbrugg were of Swiss farming stock, and hard men to beat. 'You just wouldn't argue with these two,' says Webster. 'Even the all-powerful IRTA would not dare to tell them if they were in the wrong part of the paddock. I've seen them parked in the sacred 500cc end of the paddock and no-one uttered a squeak. Just imagine doing that! Not only were they hard lads to beat, they also had a very high pain threshold. I've seen Martin racing with a gash on his leg that would have had me in bed for weeks but he shrugged it off as a graze. I was very impressed by this. I'm a secret wimp where my health is concerned! I used to be fascinated by Alfred as he had this unusual riding style. I was watching him once leading a Grand Prix at the Nurburgring and he'd got a funny little habit of sitting bolt upright just before he braked; it was just as if he was telling everyone "I'm going to brake ...NOW!" I was so busy watching him I was losing places.

Very sadly, Martin was badly injured; they had been trying to overtake Alain Michel on the start and finish straight in Austria. Alain had got a bad start and Alfred and Martin were trying to go round him, but they got it wrong, flipped the outfit over, hit the pit wall and Martin was seriously hurt. They are a great loss to the sport.'

An equally colourful pair are the Egloff twins. Webster grins saying: 'Never play tricks on these two. They have a thriving side-line in large exploding rockets. There are rockets and there are Egloff rockets – a sort of Scud version of a firework! They are confirmed practical jokers. They really took umbrage when we were racing at Donington and the sky was peppered with aircraft. They couldn't accept that something was more supreme than an Egloff missile and immediately tried to blast the aeroplanes out of the sky with their fireworks!

'So, a word of warning: beware if flying out of East Midlands airport during the British GP! Joking apart, here are two good lads who I would tip for a Grand Prix win in the near future and I know that Keith Huewen and Julian Ryder agree. The boys, pranks apart, are rated highly in the sport. Their current problem seems to be that they run out of steam halfway through a race. I can't understand this as they are both very fit. They train hard and do a lot of running – which all helps in the firework season! – do not smoke and are virtually teetotal. Steve Abbott says this is their downfall, they don't drink enough! But I do hope that I can share the rostrum with them when they win. What a celebration that will be!'

However, not all Webster's close friends come from the sidecar class of racing. He is very friendly with fellow British hopeful Niall Mackenzie: 'I have this enduring friendship with Niall. He always seems to have time for me and whenever I've had cause to celebrate, he's been there. When I was awarded the MBE, Niall went to the trouble of organizing a surprise champagne buffet in the Lucky Strike hospitality enclosure. He really made the occasion special for me. He is a lad with his feet on the ground, whereas a lot of the 500 lads don't even know who I am, let alone talk to me. Eddie Lawson said "Hello" to me once, but I think it was a mistake. Kevin Schwantz tells me that Lawson is a great bloke away from the track and I'd love to get to know him. I once asked Niall what he'd do if he couldn't race anymore. Niall is really philosophical and said that he'd be grateful for all the racing he has had and the pleasant lifestyle that it brings; then he'd get on and find a job. He would as well – he's really down to earth. I admire his attitude and his talent.'

Also greatly admired by Steve are Kevin Schwantz and Randy Mamola. 'Kevin and Randy both have a wicked sense of humour and both work tirelessly for charity. Randy has an exceptional appetite for practical jokes and he's the man who buys rockets from the Egloffs. He entertained himself at Paul Ricard by planting rockets under motorhomes and detonating them in the dead of night. Most competitors accepted this as American humour, but not Mick. No-one was going to put rockets under his van and live. Mick purchased several potent Egloff incendiaries and sought revenge. It then became a battle of nerves as to who would get the last laugh. It nearly was the last laugh as well. I think after planting the device Randy thought better of it; he must have remembered that petrol and fireworks don't mix, and at the last minute hammered like hell on the van door. We woke up just in time to feel the van rocking from the force of the explosion. My dad conceded defeat and mused: 'Well, it was nice of him to wake us up!"

'Randy Mamola, however, does not spend all his spare time larking about. He has worked devotedly for the Save the Children fund and has been responsible for organizing the now annual Day of Champions event, held either at Brands or Donington, where, for a nominal entry fee, the public are allowed into the hallowed

GP paddock and can catch a glimpse of their heroes. The event takes place in October and gives the riders an opportunity to relax with their fans, the pressures of the GP season behind them. At these functions you can get your burger cooked by Kevin Schwantz, race Randy Mamola round the track with a supermarket trolley, and of course if you are a lucky competition winner, ride on a sidecar.

'Randy is the driving force behind this jamboree, which raises thousands of pounds. He has also devoted a lot of time to a project providing motorcycles to the Third World in order to improve communications and the flow of vital supplies. A mischievous fellow with a heart of gold.'

It may seem from the anecdotes related that the GP circus has more than its fair share of would-be clowns. But this is not entirely true. Here we have people who dice with death daily as part of their job. There's a great deal of adrenalin buzzing around in the system at the end of a practice day, and all these high jinks are one way of channelling that energy. It can be a lonely life caught up in the Grand Prix merry-go-round; relationships that are formed tend to be very intense. These riders spend half the year together, where life can be glamorous but it can also be very hard.

Sacrifices also have to be made. Two people who have sacrificed a lot for Steve's progress have undoubtedly been his father, Mick, and Mick's long-time girlfriend and coerced team co-ordinator Mary Smith.

'There's no doubt at all that I wouldn't be World Champion now if it hadn't been for my father,' states Steve; 'as soon as he knew I was interested in racing he encouraged me all he could. He never pushed me into racing, it was completely my own decision, but once he saw the enthusiasm was there, nothing was too much trouble. He has helped me to make all the choices along the way, he is level-headed in a crisis and he is the still small voice of calm that I so often need.'

Racing comes first with the family Webster and because of this devotion to duty, domestic issues very often get pushed to one side. Mary has to be praised for never complaining when there are engine parts in the kitchen and wardrobes don't get built because the bike needs a rebuild. Mary has gone along to all the Grands Prix in recent years and has taken care of all the day-to-day running of the team. During the winter of 1991 it became clear to Mary that the team were going to be short of funds for the 1992 season. So with no further ado she returned to work at the Gas Board. By so doing she saved the team a salary during the winter months before returning to the team for the start of the new season. 'She never complains, she just gets on with the job! She deserves a very big "thank you", and perhaps one day I'll be able to pay her back, and I don't just mean in financial terms,' Steve claims.

Another lady lending her support, but very much in the background, is Steve's wife Karen. Throughout the early years of their relationship Karen survived on a shoestring budget to enable Steve to pursue his racing. She kept her job at Rowntrees on to finance the household expenses and to supplement the racing budget.

Like Mary she never complains and is 110 per cent behind Steve. They married in 1987 and they spent their honeymoon at the Paris conference. They must have been made for each other because Karen thoroughly enjoyed it! They now have two children, Holly and Simon. 'Since we've been together,' confesses Steve, 'life has revolved totally around me. Selfish in a way, I guess. When I retire it'll be Karen's turn. I am very lucky and I know it.'

Most people are easy to categorize into Friends or Rivals, but when it comes to the media it's a bit of a double-edged sword. 'Often articles in the press attribute things to me that I've never even thought, let alone said,' declares Steve. 'If the remarks don't actually hurt anyone or do any harm, I usually don't protest – after all, any coverage is better than none. I wouldn't want to alienate myself and get no exposure at all. I am thankful for the coverage I get, I just wish it was more! But sadly, the best coverage you seem to get is if you hurt yourself!

One classic occasion was an ACU press conference in London in 1989. There we were, four World Champions: me, Fogarty, Wigg and Thorpe. We all went down to this luxury hotel just off Fleet Street complete with our bikes and leathers. How many journalists were there to interview such a galaxy of stars? One! To make matters worse, he'd only come because he'd spotted the bikes in the car park. After this journalist, Leslie Nichol, had extensively interviewed us in this exclusive situation, we wended our way to the gents to get changed.

'"You know what we should do now, lads?" I suggested, "we should get on our bikes in our underpants and blast down Fleet Street!" That would have made these literary "friends" sit up and take notice. What a gift of a headline: "The bare-faced cheek of World Champion bikers!" If we'd had a few more beers I think we'd have done it. I accept that sidecar racing ranks somewhere around the same star status as tiddlywinks and hang-gliding. I used to get really cheesed off about it, but now I accept it. I think it will help now that Bernie Ecclestone is involved. I'm sure he'll raise our status.'

There are, however, some journalists who go out of their way to help. Mat Oxley is one, who always has a sympathetic ear for the sidecar fraternity, as does Norrie White. Locally, John Mackenzie works tirelessly to produce press releases and to bring us into the public gaze with his excellent photographic coverage.

In the final analysis, Steve finds that maintaining friends with his racing lifestyle is very difficult: 'It is hard to switch on and off, especially if you don't see people very often. You see your mates at the local during the winter and then don't see them for six months. Striking a balance is important, as you tend to put everything into racing and the sacrifices are great. It sometimes seems like reaching for a pot of gold that's balanced on the top of a hill. You must get it and in order to get it there are things you'll inevitably knock down. I've been a b*****d sometimes and I'm sorry. If I'd put as much effort into a business as I have into racing I think I could have succeeded whatever it was ... selling eggs to chickens even! Sometimes it's the greatest sport in the world, but sometimes I ask, "Is it worth it?"

'At the moment I feel it is, but if ever the answer comes back doubtfully, that's when Webbo will hang up his helmet.'

11

Counting the Cost

'There are easier ways to make money,' announces Webster; 'if I'd put as much effort into a business as I've put into racing I'm sure I'd be a millionaire by now!' Since 1984 Steve's only source of income has been racing. It was a brave decision to make it a career rather than a hobby, but certainly one which has proved to be the right decision. In the early days, he confesses to being a 'kept man'. Girlfriend Karen worked at Rowntree-Mackintosh to maintain their shared home and to top up the racing budget. Father Mick helped all he could, and Mick's long-time girlfriend Mary even offered to sell her car to add to racing finances. In more recent times, as already recorded, when sponsors disappeared over the winter months, Mary returned to work to help the team. Part of Steve's success has come from the backing he has had from family and sponsors, and part from the fact that he is a reasonable manager with his finances. He has never fallen into the pit of spending what he hasn't got and he has never asked his family to go without in order to finance the racing. Although he now has a luxury home on the outskirts of York and owns three cars, he does not live a superstar's lifestyle: he has a modest taste and his fame has left him unchanged.

'In the early days we lived a hand-to-mouth existence so that I could race. Now I am a family man with responsibilities and I would never sell my house to continue racing. Once it ceases to provide an income or I lose the will to win, I shall look for another outlet,' Webster states.

To keep a World Championship sidecar team on the track takes more than just money, although obviously a great deal of financial support is essential. The basic costs involved in 1992 were about

£15,000 for a new LCR outfit, plus £18,000 for each Krauser or ADM engine. In addition a reliable and presentable transporter can add anything from £5,000 to upwards of £50,000 to the budget. Naturally, the bike, engines and transporter have a resale value, so these costs can be spread over several seasons, or the resale values can be deducted from the total costs to arrive at an annual estimate of budget requirement. To arrive at Steve's estimate of £150,000 to £200,000 to contest a World Championship season one has to look much deeper into the equation, and realize just how fragile the modern racing machine is compared with its road-going counterpart.

The Krauser and ADM engines are four-cylinder two-strokes of 498cc and they rev to 13,000rpm to produce 150–160bhp. In doing so they wear out very rapidly! Piston life is 200 to 300 miles and crankshaft bearings last for about the same period. The cranks themselves need careful rebuilding every 500 miles, and the cylinders are coated with Nikasil, which means that they cannot be rebored and need replacing every three or four races at a cost of several thousand pounds. The seven-plate clutch will normally permit the rider to make three or four racing starts, but it is normal practice to replace it more frequently to avoid problems. Exhaust systems and reed valve blocks are changed to suit different circuits, so it is necessary to have several complete systems on hand. Additionally, the reed petals themselves become weak after a few hundred miles and have to be replaced to prevent the performance from dropping off.

All the above mileages are the maximum safe life of the components. If a mistake is made in assembling a component or if the carburation is slightly off, the resultant blow-up can reduce an £18,000 engine to a piece of useless scrap metal in seconds! It is in this area that the experienced competitor gains over his inexperienced rivals: by avoiding the silly but costly mistakes a competitor like Steve Webster can save thousands of pounds over the course of a season. Pre-event testing is expensive, circuit hire, time off work and wear and tear on the machine all cost money, but arriving at a fast but reliable set-up in private testing can avoid the costly blow-ups that afflict many competitors on race day.

Steve likes to get his basic set-up finalized before the season starts. He tests all his components privately before the first race of the season, so ensuring that he will be able to run at a competitive pace with a machine which will last to the end of the race. Private testing can be a very expensive affair as the cost of hiring a racing circuit for your exclusive use can amount to several thousand pounds per day.

One of the other unseen costs which has a major influence on the total cost of competing is the amount of travel required to reach the Grand Prix venues. Anyone who has taken a car or bike abroad will be aware of the high cost of using ferries to reach the Continent, so imagine having to pay for a substantial-sized truck and four people every two or three weeks! The truck itself costs a fair amount of money as it has to be kept up to scratch mechanically and the cost of diesel fuel is a not inconsiderable sum when taken over the year, as it is used for every continental Grand Prix. For the events in America, Brazil and Malaysia the outfit is crated-up and flown to its destination.

Steve is very fortunate in having Avon and Silkolene as his major sponsors. The cost of tyres has increased dramatically over the last few years, but because Steve has carried out much of Avon's testing in recent years, he knows which tyre compound to use in any given set of circumstances. Furthermore, these tyres are supplied free of charge by Avon as part of his sponsorship. Yet, fuel is a different matter altogether. Silkolene supply the Webster equipe with all their lubricants, from the essential competition two-stroke oil to chain lubricant. They do not, however, produce petrol. The highly tuned engines require a very special fuel which must be of a high octane to produce power, but must also burn coolly to prevent the engine detonating and overheating. Many alternatives have been tried in the never-ending quest for the perfect fuel mix. The French oil giant, Elf, produce a special fuel aimed at the two-stroke competitor called Moto 119, or 'Bluegas'. As its name implies, it is rated at 119 octane, compared with pump four-star at 98 octane. This toxic brew sells for about £5 per litre or £25 per gallon! An alternative is to mix aviation fuel (Avgas) with petrol, but unfortunately this solution is now illegal in the UK and many other European countries due to the high lead content of Avgas. Over the course of a season the racing outfit will consume its fuel at a rate of one gallon every 10 miles, so at £25 per gallon this can mount up to a sizeable sum!

A final consideration for the sidecar competitor is the cost of keeping the team in food and the other mundane essentials of life, such as beer!

Compared with most other forms of motorsport, the budget required to run a competitive sidecar outfit in the World Championship is low. A Formula One car racing team needs at least £15 million to function for the year; the major 500cc solo teams could not operate as they do on much less than £2 million pounds; a Formula Three car running in the British Championship costs £300,000, a top contender in the British Saloon Car Championship £500,000. At only £150,000 a sidecar must represent good value for money to a potential sponsor, and if more sponsors realized this maybe there would be a rush to support this most exciting branch of the sport, which, until they do, will remain the Cinderella of the motorsport world!

To achieve any degree of success in any branch of motorsport requires talent. To achieve consistent success requires adequate finance to complement that talent. Without sponsorship motorsport, as we know it, would disappear completely. At the rarefied levels of Formula One and 500cc Grand Prix motorcycling, only the tobacco companies seem to have the amount of money needed to keep the show on the road. If the European Community ban cigarette advertising through sports sponsorship, as they are trying to do, the effects on motorsport will be absolutely catastrophic! Without the vast input from the cigarette companies, nearly every major team on two and four wheels will cease to exist. Apart from Egbert Streuer's Lucky Strike sponsorship, the cigarette manufacturers have not become involved with the sidecar racers, so perhaps in this respect, this form of the sport will suffer less than most.

Getting sponsors interested is like searching for the Holy Grail. In the past Steve has employed marketing experts to prepare portfolios for him. 'I imagined people would pursue a World Champion and be begging me to let them sponsor me ... if only.' But any sponsors that have come Steve's way have been as a result of personal contact. Finding someone who gets to know you and really believes in your talent, wanting you to succeed, is better than a lorry load of portfolios. But there are some who have helped Steve. 'I would never have got anywhere at all if it hadn't have been for Paul Seward. He put me on the right track with my racing and he has always had his ear to the ground to find other backers. He showed us how to have a professional approach and how to present ourselves as a worthwhile package. He got us started and he still helps now, although not financially, but he would if circumstances allowed. However, he has introduced us to many other sources of finance.'

It was Paul Seward who introduced Steve to the Brown brothers, for whose input Steve will be eternally grateful: 'They really treated me like a World Champion. Nothing was too much trouble. They rewarded our efforts with holidays in Norway, where they really made us feel VIPs. They would take us around the Broyt factory there and we'd feel real celebrities. They were totally committed to the sport. I wish they'd get something going and we could have another crack. I still see both Ron and Gordon quite often. They were here to celebrate my fourth World Championship win,' Steve reports.

Other sponsors who have stuck with Steve through thick and thin are Avon and Silkolene. 'These are two sponsors who do not pull the rug out from under you if you happen to have a bad season. In fact, when we lost the Championship in 1990, Avon gave me more money to try to help my efforts for 1991. There is a lot of respect between Avon and myself, and I'd like to take this opportunity to thank them. We have a friendship that goes on and on. Silkolene also are generous sponsors and I am grateful to have been running with their name in 1992. They have not faltered despite all the uncertainty surrounding the sport at present.'

When Browns collapsed, in 1990, Roland Munch stepped in. But Roland was very worried by the lack of a definite calendar for 1992. 'I do hope,' said Steve early in the year, 'that we have an appealing package to offer him in the coming season. We've sent him faxes saying: "Merry Christmas", "Happy New Year" and "How are you?" etc, but what he really needs is, "This is the calendar, Roland", and who can blame him?!'

Another sponsor who stepped in, in Webster's hour of need, was BSB Television. Steve is grateful to journalist Paul Fowler for pointing out Steve's predicament on satellite TV and for getting BSB interested. Donnie McCloud also did a sterling job especially during his commentary at Assen when he stressed: 'Here is Steve

Webster and Tony Hewitt, both of whom hold the MBE. Their sponsors have gone bust, but surely someone can help them?' The BSB support enabled Steve and Gavin to continue their attack on the 1990 World crown.

Steve is also indebted to Dennis Trollope for his generous support: 'I feel Dennis and I will always have a connection. Who knows where the new structure under Bernie Ecclestone will lead us all? Dennis helped me a lot, and I will always reflect some of his influence in my driving style.'

Few Webster fans will have failed to notice the Levior helmets sported by Steve and his passenger. 'Over the years, Levior have supported us,' said Steve early in 1992, 'and we have been proud to wear their helmets. Unfortunately, their helmets are presently not legal in Britain, although they should be from May due to changes in European law.' At that stage, Steve was still hopeful that once he could show them the elusive race calendar, the association would continue, but Levior were not the only potential sponsor to develop cold feet due to the vagueness of the 1992 season. 'I had a deal underway with a large British company, but due to the uncertainty surrounding the calendar they have deferred making their decision but will probably support us from the start of 1993, providing that the sport has sorted itself out. It has been a winter of discontent.'

However, not all the rewards in racing are of the financial nature. One of the most memorable days of Steve's career was the day that he and Tony trouped off to Buckingham Palace to receive their MBEs. 'At first I thought this was a wind-up,' admits Steve. 'John Webb had said to me, "Don't you be surprised if you get an award soon; it's nearly the Birthday Honours list, you know." I took this to be a joke and I confess that when an official letter arrived saying that the Prime Minister had it in mind to submit my name to the Queen for inclusion in the Birthday Honours list, I still suspected practical jokers. However, I filled in the form saying I was agreeable, and the next thing I knew I was being approached by journalists saying they'd had a press release with the Webster and Hewitt names on it. In June 1990, Tony and I received the invitation to go to the investiture at the Palace. It was amazingly exciting. We went along and it was a real experience. First you are there in the hustle and bustle of London, and then you are ushered into the Quadrangle of the Palace. You are aware that you are now in a special place where members of the public are not allowed to go – bit like a GP paddock! I felt really special and really nervous. We were told where to go – recipients to the left, guests to the right. I had never seen so many huge paintings in all my life, they covered every wall.

'As Tony and I were getting our awards in a pair, we had to rehearse a special way of walking. We had to walk together, take seven steps, turn, walk three steps, bow and wait. It didn't occur to me to giggle, not even when the orchestra in the gallery struck up a tune as we marched along. I was truly overwhelmed. When we actually saw the Queen our legs turned to jelly. I was extremely impressed by Her Majesty's knowledge of our sport. She asked us how sidecars had changed since she was a girl and she obviously knew quite a bit about us, she told us how well we had done. It sent a shiver down your spine, but it made you feel it was great to be British.

'I'm not sure who nominated us for the MBE. I think it has to be a politician, so it may well have been Colin Moynihan in his role as Minister for Sport. He had enjoyed a ride round on a lap of honour with us when we'd won the British GP at Donington in 1989. If it was, because I've never been able to find out, let me say "Thank you, it really is an honour".'

Even Steve's bank responded with congratulations. 'They've always enjoyed writing to me,' quips Steve, 'but this letter is a bit different from the ones I used to get!'

When considering 'counting the cost', there is also the cost of people's lives to consider. As mentioned in Chapter 10, there are times when the ultimate price is paid in the name of sport. 'This year all my nightmares have turned to reality,' laments Steve; 'I will be haunted by the death of my friend Graham Rose for ever. He would not want me to give up racing because of the events of that sad day in October 1991; he loved the sport just as I do. Similarly with Derek Bayley, a life ruined. Sometimes the cost cannot be counted or quantified.'

12

The Crown Regained

Webster prepared for the 1991 season with a renewed fire coursing through his veins. 'Do you know,' he muses, 'I'd been at the top for so long, I'd forgotten how much I hate to be beaten. I was determined to rise from the ashes in 1991 and wrestle the title back from my friend and rival Alain Michel!'

1991 opened with Webster in fighting form. He had realized that he'd allowed complacency to creep in a little in 1989 and that, coupled with the fragility of sidecar engines, had led to the World crown being taken across the Channel. 'I'd always had a good record where reliability was concerned,' states Steve, 'but the hammer that the engine has to take is tremendous and in 1990 the mechanical difficulties just overtook me at the end of the season.'

'I welcomed the "drop your two worst scores rule" for '91 as it did reduce the luck element in race points accumulation.' In fact, there was no need to have worried about the 1991 season at all. Steve had never had control of a Championship in the way that he had from those five wins from five finishes at the beginning of that season.

It began for the sidecar contestants at Laguna Seca. The 500cc riders had had their usual forays to Japan and Australia, but round one for the sidecars was in America. 'Conditions at Laguna Seca are a great leveller,' smiles Steve; 'the 500 boys end up sharing facilities and there are more tents than hospitality units.'

Practice at Laguna was full of incident. 'The track seemed to echo with the sound of cracking collarbones,' Steve says, grimacing. 'Eggy was using his friend and part-time passenger "Harry from behind the bar". I'm not clear what had gone off between Eggy and Gerald De Haas, but Harry's appearance was a surprise to us all. It was also a brief appearance as poor Harry fell out in practice and broke his collarbone. Egbert quickly arranged for Peter Essaff, an American sidecar driver, to take the chair. Meanwhile, my friend Rolf had broken his collarbone, but this didn't mean he wasn't racing! And the race itself? Well, it was a bit worrying at first,' recalls Webster, 'as Alain and Simon were on pole. There's always something a bit psychological about getting pole, or not getting pole as the case may be, but Alain dropped to second very quickly with brake problems. We are the only team to run AP carbon brakes and on this occasion they were worth their weight in gold. Alain's brakes had got hot and he had to ease off until they cooled down, so this gave us the chance to sneak into the lead. However, Michel/Birchall still claimed fastest lap. Poor Egbert dropped out with gear linkage problems – it really wasn't his weekend! We'd done well, but it wasn't us that the British fans were talking about after that race, it was the cracking result put in by the Dixons, on the rostrum in third place, having kept wily old fox Biland at bay in their first Grand Prix!'

The season had got off to a pleasing start for the Yorkshire pair and the team looked forward to the round in Spain with enthusiasm. 'You can't help getting excited about Spain, not that the track is anything to shout about, but the fans are brilliant. Following Jorge "Aspar" Martinez is a religion, and a crowd of over 200,000 lined the track on race day. Certainly the atmosphere got us all fired up. Also, Avon had developed a special hard front tyre for this track which complemented our AP carbon brakes superbly. We were really on song. We smashed the circuit record for sidecars and cruised in to our second win of the season,' glows Steve. It was not such a happy day for Michel and Streuer though. Alain had qualified on pole, but problems at the start made him feel the race would be stopped. Both he and Eggy got boxed-in in the ensuing mayhem, and collided with each other. They both finished out of the points and Webster and Simmons shared the rostrum with some of the sport's rising stars, ex-karters Paul and Charly Guedel and the well-liked British pair Abbott and Smith.

'As we travelled to Italy for the next round at Misano, I had to spend quite a bit of time trying to cheer up my friend Alain Michel. He had felt that the decision regarding the start at Jerez was the wrong one and he was feeling rather down in the dumps. Although we are rivals on the track, you do get very close to people when you spend seven months of the year travelling about with them. Naturally, everyone is there to win, but you don't like to see your friends feeling demotivated. I tried my best to get him into positive mode, but for Alain and Simon, Misano, in Italy was another disappointment. They led for the first five laps and then fell foul of a slow puncture. Eventually Alain pitted for a fresh tyre, but retired soon after with clutch failure. Meanwhile, we were easing into the lead having overtaken Alain on lap six. Biland, the pole sitter – we were second on the grid – had also retired with clutch trouble. Egbert, still with Peter Essaff "temporarily" in the chair, was battling it out with the Guedels and eventually came in a nifty second. It is noticeable with the Guedels – and I don't know why – that they do seem to tire near the end of a race. If they had kept up their early blistering pace in Misano they would have made it to second easily. However, I do predict that it won't be long before they have a GP win. A pair to watch, but not from behind; they are so precise it makes me dizzy!'

Webster had now clocked up three wins from three finishes. In Italy he cruised in with an enviable 14-second lead. Webster and Simmons also added another lap record to their ever growing collection by beating Biland/Waltisperg's previous 1min 20.135sec record to make it 1min 20.039sec in the record books. However, success does not last forever: 'Well, it had to happen, didn't it?' muses Webster; 'Things were going just a bit too smoothly!'

At the German GP the British pair of sidecar superstars had qualified on pole, nearly 6/10ths of a second ahead of local butcher Ralph Bohnhorst. However, the local pair got ahead, but ran their outfit into the dirt on lap seven. Both Webster and Streuer, close behind, caught some of the dust thrown up by Bohnhorst and Hiller and ultimately this dust caused Webster's engine to seize on lap 10. 'I was leading when the engine seized, and before anyone even thinks it, I have heard all the "local butcher makes mincemeat of Webbo" jokes, thank you! Seriously, Bohnhorst is very impressive and I think we'll hear more of him.' Bohnhorst and Hiller's victory made it three German wins that day, with Waldmann the victor in the 125 race and Bradl in the 250. British fans will welcome the day when three British victories can be cheered at Donington.

By the time that the GP merry-go-round came to rest at the Salzburgring, in Austria, Webster was feeling under par. 'Ever since I had problems with my stomach as a child,' says Steve, 'if I pick up a bug now, it really lays me low. I'd manged to catch a stomach virus whilst we were in Austria and I actually had to miss final qualifying. I was determined to race, but I was in real pain. The events that took place at the start of the race made me feel even more physically sick. There was a horrendous pile up at the start, resulting in very serious injuries to Martin Zurbrugg. I'd always admired the Zurbruggs for their toughness. I'd seen Martin come off the outfit with his toe literally half worn away because he'd been scraping it on the track during the course of the race. His boot had been destroyed and his toe was a mess of blood and pulp. This would have had me in hospital for weeks, but Martin shrugged it off as a scratch. Nevertheless, the human body is fragile and we are not designed to stand high-impact smashes against metal barriers and concrete, and this is what happened to poor Martin on that day in Austria. I was on pole, despite missing final qualifying, Alain was beside me, with Rolf in third position. The last two practice sessions had been wet, so the grid was very much a hotch potch, having been born from a selection of not very reliable lap times.

'I was feeling lousy and just wanted to get the race over and lie down. Alain's clutch failed at the start and the Zurbruggs, determined to do well, shot from the sixth row, got boxed in and slammed into Alain's machine. They ran up over the back of the machine and flipped the outfit over onto the pit wall, and then rebounded on to the outfit of Tony Baker and Simon Prior, who miraculously weren't hurt. Both Alfred and Martin were injured, Martin the most seriously, with a badly broken pelvis and Alfred with damaged ankle ligaments. I think the fact that they were so fit and really tough outdoor types helped them to recover. A less fit person could have died from the sort of injuries Martin sustained because the effect of the shock alone would have caused great problems for a person not trained as an athletic sportsman. Martin has recovered, I'm delighted to say, but he has not made a complete recovery yet and certainly won't race again. Alfred retired from racing that day, because although his recovery was complete, he'd had one brush with fate and wasn't inviting another. One's mortality is very fragile and you just can't dwell on the dangers when you are racing or you simply wouldn't do it, or at any rate, you wouldn't do it competitively. But that risk is always there, and we were all very shaken by what had happened that day at the Salzburgring.'

The race was re-run after a long delay but Alain Michel did not rejoin. Not only was his outfit damaged but he was also too shaken to want to race that day. Webster got away perfectly, shooting into the lead and staying there. Again, a local pair were in contention, this time the Austrians Klaffenbock and Parzer. Unfortunately, much to the dismay of the crowd who were nearly hoarse from yelling encouragement, the Austrian lads got into a monumental slide at the first chicane and collected the British pair of Abbott and Smith. The battle for second was fast and furious between Kumano, Klaffenbock, the Guedels, Bohnhorst and Abbott, as two seconds covered this entire rabble! Biland seized the opportunity to nip into second place on the last lap, having worked his way up from 11th on lap one, but Webster was long gone, 15 seconds ahead of the other 'worms'.

The next scheduled event on the calendar was to have been the Yugoslavian Grand Prix at the Rijeka circuit. The political upheaval in Central Europe leading to the demise of hard-line Communism had been achieved relatively peacefully, but the transition in Yugoslavia had boiled over into civil war. The teams and riders had never been particularly fond of the Rijeka circuit and had been putting pressure on the FIM from the start of the season to cancel the visit to Yugoslavia. The FIM prevaricated for far too long, hoping that the political situation would stabilize and allow the Grand Prix to take place, but eventually sense prevailed, and just three weeks before the event it was switched to the Jarama circuit in Spain. This was not a popular decision, however, due to the amount of travelling involved. The newly revised schedule meant that there were three races in 23 days involving long road journeys from Austria to Spain and then back to the other end of Europe, to Holland.

The enthusiasm of the Spanish for bike racing was underlined yet again when the circuit at Jarama ran out of tickets for the Grand Prix of Europe event. It was estimated that in addition to the 60,000 spectators who did pay, at least 10,000 entered the circuit by devious routes.

'The heat was incredible,' remembers Webster, 'it certainly made you sweat a bit!' he grins. The sidecar race was in fact shortened to 20 laps because of the heat. Webster and Simmons managed to put the LCR firmly in pole position with a lap of 1min 39.267sec, but the opening lap was very hair-raising! 'Klaffenbock was a shade over-enthusiastic,' remarks Webster, 'he tends to suffer a bit from the old red haze syndrome and he nearly put me off on the way into turn one. It was another moment of glory for my ace brakes as I was able to outbrake him, but the old heart certainly missed a beat!' Klaffenbock is definitely not afraid to throw his outfit around, and he wrestled the lead back by chucking his chair into turn two. Meanwhile, Webster was under pressure from the ever precise Guedels, but he sensibly hung back for a few laps and waited for the chance to pounce!

The opening came on lap five: Webster powered into the lead and was never troubled again. 'I've learned a lot over the years,' philosophizes the World Champion; 'There was a hell of a lot of sorting out going on in lap four, and at one time of the day I'd have been in there fighting for every inch. I know now that races are not won on the first corner and there is a lot to be gained by clear thinking and a few tactics.'

The day ended with five Britons on the rostrum: Webster, Simmons, Birchall, Abbott and Smith. A great day, even though the heat was enervating. Webster had 100 points in the bag, so he could pat himself on the back, but the battle was not yet over.

'It's no secret that I have a serious regard for Biland's talents. To see him nosing into second place did make the hairs on my neck bristle. I snatched the Championship from under Biland's nose in 1988, but the same could happen to me. I had the germ of this little worry in my mind and it began to flourish as the season progressed. The events at the next round at Assen tipped Rolf off to the fact that he had a straight-line speed disadvantage, and he set out to remedy this with frightening thoroughness,' says Steve.

At Assen the weather conditions were appalling and constantly changing. 'We must have had the outfit out there in every conceivable weather condition bar snow,' groans Webster. 'We managed to grab pole just ahead of Eggy, but we soon retired with an engine failure. The report on Eurosport was somewhat prophetic; a lap before we pulled off Keith Huewen and Julian

Ryder were saying: "Webster is missing from the leader board, what's happened?" and they flashed on to my dad in the pits. At this point we were happily leading the race, but no sooner had their camera men rediscovered us than we stopped! I do hope that this pair have not caught the famous Murray Walker jinx!'

With Webster in the pits, British hopes focused on Steve Abbott and Shaun Smith, from Derbyshire. They were performing brilliantly and had clawed their way up to second, so perhaps it could be a British victory after all.

The crowds in front of their satellite televisions and those that were not totally deep frozen at Assen roared as Steve and Shaun took the lead on lap six, but the thrill was short-lived as Biland slid into the lead one lap later. Abbott and Smith were battling with the Guedels for second place. So it was Swiss precision versus the British bulldog spirit. Alas it all ended unhappily as, on lap 10, the British pair ran wide and the ever-accurate Swiss brothers sped past. Steve Abbott swerved to get back on line but collided with the Guedels and Shaun Smith was unceremoniously spat out on to the tarmac.

The disappointment for British fans was intense: no Webster victory and the great effort by Abbott and Smith scuppered on the 10th lap. A great race, though, and lovely to deliberate upon what might have been! Steve Abbott was characteristically philosophical about it all: 'Ay, I was much faster down the straight without him you know!'

The locals were thrilled, however, to see Streuer and his new British passenger Peter Brown cutting through the field and, having saved his tyres a little more than Biland, making a monumental effort on the 13th lap – lucky for some – to take the lead. Again a local boy wins at his home Grand Prix, so the prospect of Donington was eagerly awaited.

'By the time we all landed at Paul Ricard, Biland had been doing some very serious development work in a wind-tunnel, studying the aerodynamics of his machine to enhance his straight-line speed. This was to cause me major headaches,' grimaces Steve.

Another major headache at Paul Ricard was the saga of the starting lights. The starters were using a set of subsidiary lights as well as the main set, and many riders were caught out by watching the wrong set. Riders in all classes fell foul of these.

'I admit I didn't make a good start,' sighs Webster. 'I was fifth at the end of lap one, which isn't very impressive from pole. I tried to force my way through, but everything was cooking: clutch, tyres, brakes, brain! But even if I'd got off the line better, I doubt if I could have done a thing about Rolf for he was flying.We got up to second, but Rolf had me beaten fair and square.'

Perfect weather heralded the preparations for the British Grand Prix. The official practice day was Friday, August 2, but from Tuesday, July 30, the Grand Prix roadshow began to wind its way down the narrow and leafy Leicestershire lanes leading to the circuit. For the British teams it was a time to arrive in a relaxed manner. There were no ferries to worry about, no Customs to go through, just a leisurely drive down the M1 to friendly old Donington. But, coupled with these advantages is the pressure of doing well for your home crowd, so butterflies were stirring in the Webster stomach. Other duties also beckoned at Donington, such as presenting a new ambulance to the marshals, and taking part in phone-ins and charity events. This was all very enjoyable, but also turned up the pressure.

The first sidecar practice, late on Friday morning, set the tone for the whole meeting and reinforced the serious misgivings that Steve was feeling about the Championship. Rolf Biland was in a different class from everyone else, consistently turning laps over a second quicker than Webster, while Streuer, Michel, Abbott, Egloff and Paul Guedel were all close together, fighting over second place on the grid. To the average spectator Steve's tactics in practice were puzzling as the Webster outfit spent very little time on the circuit, instead being seen stationary in the pits for long periods whilst the team were deep in conversation. Many people may have thought that Steve and Gavin had machine problems but this was not the case. The problem was the consistent speed of the Swiss pairing. Rolf and Kurt were able to lap in the low 1min 37sec bracket at will, whereas Steve and Gavin could not get below 1min 39sec for most of the four practice sessions. They knew that their machine was working well but it was disheartening that Biland was so much quicker. All the British pair could hope for was that Biland would run into tyre or machine problems in the race if he kept up his practice times on Sunday afternoon.

In the final practice session Steve improved his time to 1min 38.132sec, compared with his own lap record of 1min 39.34sec. This was a fantastic lap, but against Biland's pole-setting lap of 1min 37.261sec, it was far from good enough. Therefore the British pairing would have to settle for second on the grid, hoping, of course, that such a position would not be a permanent feature of the race.

Sadly, this was indeed the case. Biland led from the start and at first Webster wasn't even in the frame at all. Faces of the fans began to show increasing anxiety: Redgate, the Old Hairpin and McLeans were awash with 'Go for it Webbo' banners, but Rolf was in control. Even the power of the fans' support could do nothing to alter the pecking order. Streuer was in second place and Abbott and Smith were hanging on to third. The Riddings pair had put on a new chain for the race, which proved a bad move because the chain broke on the second lap, causing them to retire and nearly causing Steve – who was right behind – to run into them! Webster and Guedel powered past Streuer, but the Guedels were soon to be dogged by mechanical problems. Webster's efforts to gain on Biland were further thwarted by a backmarker who was cluttering up the racing line as Webster tried to pass him and reel in the three-second lead that the Swiss pair now had. This was not the outcome that the fans or Webster had hoped for. With Biland's victory Webster's lead in the Championship was diminishing, and he headed for Mugello a worried man.

The circuit at Mugello is in the most delightful setting and ideal for fans who wish to combine a holiday with watching a GP. The problem with Mugello is that everything has been updated except for the roads leading to the circuit. The Avon tyre technicians were horrified that it took them five hours to travel from their hotel, 20 kilometres away, to the track on a practice day! They were eventually forced to watch Steve and Gavin practice from the roadside. The circuit is served by country lanes which are not capable of absorbing the large numbers of personnel and spectators that accompany a Grand Prix. This is a pity, as the circuit has been extensively refurbished and is in a glorious position. The track had recently been resurfaced at Mugello and in the week leading up to the Grand Prix, when the most prudent thing to do was get in the circuit and stay there, the teams had spent a lot of time pounding round the track in road cars trying to lay some rubber on the surface to make it less slippery. It still appeared to be too slippery for Klaffenbock, being a case of the old mobile accident looking for somewhere to happen. This time he hit the Dixons and shunted poor Steve Abbott out of the race.

Webster had not made a good start and this contretemps gave him time to catch up. Michel also had been slow off the line, but he was scything his way through the field. At first the Egloffs were in the lead, with Ralph Bohnhorst a confident second. Alain snatched the lead on lap five, but Steve soon took this from him and led for three laps. Meanwhile, Biland, who had qualified second, was in the pits trying to solve a carburation problem. He wished to rejoin the race – albeit six laps down – so he thought he'd lurk in the pit lane and rejoin just behind Webster. Seeing the purple outfit menacingly pull out behind him horrified Webster: 'I really thought that he was going to push me off. He'd pulled across on me at Anderstorp in '87 and I wouldn't have put it past him to have me off.' Later Biland said that he had no such ideas and Webster was over-reacting. 'I deliberately let Biland get in between myself and Alain, who was leading the race at the time,' confesses Webster. 'Gav was going mad and beating my helmet to a pulp. I wish we'd got helmet-to-helmet intercoms as he was very confused and very angry with me. All I could think was that I'd rather Alain win and we could at least finish. Gavin thought I was crazy. But on the last lap Biland pulled aside and let me past. Who knows what he really thought!

'My heart leapt as I saw Alain slowing. I thought I'd got it in the bag after all, but just at the last moment Michel and Birchall squeezed over the line, winning by 2/100ths of a second. Although he was six laps down Biland had beaten me that day.'

Once the Simmons' induced headache had cleared Steve did his sums to see what the true lie of the land really was. This was where the 'drop your two worst scores' really mattered. Webster had to finish within three points of wily Rolf to clinch his fourth World Championship title. The trip to Brno, however, was to be fraught with problems.

'We were rather worried about the political situation,' remarks Steve, 'and I don't mean the FIM, IRTA and Bernie saga. If you recall, this was just after the ousting of Gorbachev. He'd just been returned to power when we went to Brno, but I get very wary of an overwhelming presence of officialdom, and to see tanks rolling about made me very uneasy. Another factor was the absence of spectators. They simply couldn't afford to come and spectate, ticket prices being so high.'

Early on Saturday morning there was another problem. A track cleaning lorry burst a pipe and spilt oil in several places on the track. This took a good three hours to clean up. Practice was delayed, reorganized, rescheduled and generally it was chaos. 'We were sent out to lay rubber down, but of course Abbo had to tie a brush to his outfit, just to rub it in!' In fact once the initial rubber laying exercise was completed the sidecar riders did well. The later classes had torrential rain to cope with and in the end the final practice for the 250 and 500 classes was cancelled. Only the chairs and the 125s had anything like a decent amount of practice time. Still, there were further problems ahead for Webster.

'I'd had gearchange problems in practice and we just couldn't seem to get the carburation right,' exclaims Steve. 'The weather was unpredictable and we kept running into niggling little problems. I ended up qualifying sixth which was my worst position all season. It just seemed as if my chance of the Championship was slipping away.

'Eggy was on pole, but Klaffenbock stormed through from seventh to lead for two laps but he quickly retired with engine trouble. Rolf had made a bad start, but was sweeping to the front. My gearbox was still temperamental and I didn't want to slow suddenly and cause an accident, so I settled into third place. Egbert was into second and Biland was soon leading. I was willing Eggy to win. Biland was having problems getting the power on out of corners, but he hung on to take the flag. This left me in the position that I must finish 14th or higher to win the Championship at Le Mans in two weeks time. To beat me Biland had to win, with us not finishing. It sounds like good odds, but who can account for the fickle finger of fate?'

At the 'Not the Brazilian Grand Prix' – the Grand Prix de Vitesse du Mans at the Circuit du Sarthe – Webster was in fighting form. He was so close to achieving his goal. The outfit was in tiptop form with an extra large diameter rear wheel and tyre to reduce the chance of the abrasive circuit surface shaking the tyre to death.

Webster was cool and composed: 'Naturally, in the back of my mind I remembered the two breakdowns in Germany and Assen, but we had done everything we could to ensure a sound performance.'

Biland was fantastic in practice, scooping pole position with ease. Webster qualified third. Separating Rolf and Steve was friend and rival Alain Michel. Biland drove a faultless race. To Webster the 21 laps were endless, but the race was incident-free and Steve came in a steady third. The fourth World Championship title was his, and Gavin Simmons had achieved his first World crown.

Although the final run in to the title had seemed close, the statistics of the season emphasized what a brilliantly consistent performance the Yorkshire duo had put together. From the 12 rounds, Steve and Gavin had won five to Biland's four; they had finished in second place three times and in third place twice, and they had retired with mechanical problems only twice. They never finished lower than third and so were on the podium every time they finished; their final points tally was 181 points out of a possible total of 200. From the 12 rounds, Steve and Gavin sat on pole position six times and were only off the front row once, in Czechoslovakia. Surprisingly, they only set the fastest race lap in three of the 12 Grand Prix events, possibly because they established a comfortable early lead in many of the races, so that they didn't need to push in the later stages when the machines are at their quickest, thanks to the lightened fuel load.

The title had gone to a pair who richly deserved the honour. One of their sponsors, Roland Munch, profusely congratulated them and then asked, 'What next?'!

13

Winter of Discontent

After basking in the memory of his triumph of the 1991 season when the World crown was regained, Steve Webster was brought down to earth with a bump as he learned of the political chicanery that would inevitably decide his future. The words of Roland Munch at Le Mans: 'Forward, forward', haunted him all through the winter. 'Everything that I've tried to do has been thwarted by my lack of knowledge of the new Championship arrangements,' sighed Webster. 'Potential sponsors are not captivated by statements such as "Well, I'll be racing a sidecar but I don't exactly know where or when."' Speaking before the start of the new season, Steve added: 'I'm sure that when the Championship is finalized Bernie Ecclestone will do everything he can to promote sidecar racing. I know from my telephone conversations with him that he is an enthusiast. But, here we are in February and I still don't have a calendar!'

Steve recollects that there was no big announcement about the new series: 'I was approached in the paddock at Paul Ricard by a journalist who casually said, "Hey Webbo, what do you think, there's going to be an IRTA World Series and there's no chairs!"' After that he did all he could to find out what the score was, but he was still in the dark six weeks before the start of the season!

At the end of September, with the 1991 season satisfactorily completed and only the political machinations of the FIM and IRTA to detract from his fourth World Championship, Steve and his family had taken a well-earned holiday. Two weeks were spent enjoying the attractions of Tenerife; being able to spend time with his family, playing with the kids and lavishing attention on Karen, which she could never expect during the racing season, it all seemed idyllic. Being an 'unknown' superstar has its benefits and the World Champion's family were able to enjoy their holiday like any normal holidaymakers.

Although Steve was aware of the threat of a breakaway World Series, he thought that it was just another muscle-flexing exercise by those parties involved in the struggle to control road racing. He assumed that it would all be resolved by the time he got home and he didn't really think about the possible threat to his career; it didn't seem at all real, so he just concentrated on enjoying his holiday and the novelty of time to spend with his wife and children. During his vacation he remained out of touch with racing and blissfully unaware of the major rows that were brewing between the FIM and IRTA.

However, on his return to Easingwold, Steve's first thought was to check what had arrived in the post during his absence. In amongst the messages of congratulations and the inevitable bills were two copies of *Motor Cycle News*, the weekly 'bible' of the motorcycling fraternity. The banner headline 'WORLD SERIES IS GO' stopped him dead in his tracks, for as he read the front page article he began to realize that the paddock rumours had come true. The article clearly stated that Paul Butler of IRTA had signed an agreement with Formula One car mogul Bernie Ecclestone to set up a professional road-race series for all the solo classes. The bad news for Steve was that there would be no place for the sidecars. As he stood in his hallway he saw the other lead article on the front page: 500cc champ Wayne Rainey had badly broken his leg in a practice crash at Shah Allam. Steve thought that the motorcycling world would be short of two World Champions: Rainey for a few months whilst his leg healed and Webster out of racing forever, thanks to his supposed friends at IRTA!

As Steve regained his composure he glanced at the second copy of *Motor Cycle News*. It's headline read 'WRECKED! – World Series bid is scuppered as Ecclestone signs TV deal with FIM'. Webster was as confused as the rest of the motorcycling community although there was a glimmer of hope in the article as it stated that the sidecars would be included in the new arrangements.

To try to understand all this confusion one needs to take a close look at the way motorcycle road racing has evolved over the past decade and to study the characters involved, their motivations and loyalties.

The Federation Internationale Motorcycliste (FIM), is the governing body of all forms of motorcycle sport. It is made up of elected representatives from every country where motorcycle sport is practised. The road racing sub-committee (CCR) is comprised of senior members of the FIM, circuit owners, and in recent years, representatives from the teams and riders. It is the CCR which formulates rules and carries out the day-to-day running of Grand Prix racing. As the sport evolved from a mainly amateur competition to the serious professionalism of the 1980s, the major players in the 500cc class demanded a far larger say in the running of the sport. Organizations were formed to represent the interests of the teams, riders and promoters. Many of these organizations are very professional, staffed by such people as experienced lawyers and advertising and marketing executives. Clashes between the enthusiastic amateur (ie unpaid) officials of the FIM and the commercial interests of the large teams and their multi-national sponsors was inevitable.

The first rumblings of discontent started in the late 1970s when the riders, led by Kenny Roberts and Barry Sheene, formed themselves into a group to put pressure on the organizers to pay them a more realistic amount and to improve the safety facilities at many circuits. When the race organizers proved reluctant to comply with their requests, the riders threatened to form a breakaway group. It was here that World Series was conceived. Eventually peace broke out and the two groups reached an accommodation. The riders continued to run in the FIM Grands Prix, and the World Series was quietly pushed to one side, but it had not been forgotten!

In the 1980s the major Japanese factories increased their involvement. The huge tobacco companies were attracted into the sport and the teams became big organizations: the sport had evolved into a multi-million pound entertainment industry. The sponsors needed major television coverage to justify their involvement as television would bring even more money into racing. With it came the army of marketeers, promoters, managers and PR executives that are essential to modern professional sport.

Although the FIM were still the governing authority, they gradually lost their day-to-day control to the International Race Teams Association (IRTA), who took over such things as the organization of the paddock, issue of passes and scheduling of events. The promotion and marketing of events passed to the promoters' association (ROPA), who endeavoured to gain television coverage for the individual Grands Prix. With so many different organizations being involved in the running of Grand Prix meetings, it is not surprising that conflicts of interest were always arising, and that the various parties did not wish to confide in one another.

For the last few years it has been obvious to anyone in the sport that the FIM and IRTA were on a collision course. Their aims and objectives were not compatible and the struggle for control of the sport was no longer hidden. Both parties were openly shaping up for the inevitable confrontation.

The press would have us believe that the core of the then current dispute rested in the FIM's attempt to reassert its authority by introducing new regulations to replace the current factory V4 two-strokes with a four-stroke engine formula. The FIM made this announcement in mid-season, apparently without first discussing it with IRTA, who claimed to represent not just the teams, but the factories themselves. This was no doubt the catalyst that IRTA had been waiting for and they dismissed the new regulations as being unacceptable to them, to the factories and to the riders. IRTA announced that it would press ahead with its own plans and reintroduced the concept of World Series. They also announced that they had the backing of Bernie Ecclestone, who would be responsible for the promotion and television rights to their reborn prodigy.

Although the press and IRTA maintained that it was the FIM who precipitated the conflict, with the proposed change to the regulations, the fairer assessment was probably that both parties left themselves open to manipulation, and this had led to the ultimate disintegration of the Grand Prix series.

In 1988 the FIM signed a contract with Bernie Ecclestone. They had seen how Ecclestone's companies had promoted Formula One car racing through television, and they thought that Bernie could do the same for the bike Grands Prix. For reasons unclear the FIM cancelled its deal with Ecclestone in 1990 and awarded the television rights to the Spanish company, Dorna. Whatever the reason behind this move, the effect was to antagonize Bernie Ecclestone and to leave him with the desire to regain the television rights, and to claim a bigger slice of motorcycle racing at the same time. Ecclestone is a shrewd businessman, a self-made millionaire with the best track record in motorsport promotion that the world has ever seen. He can also be a formidable adversary, as the FIM have now found out. His years in the car racing world have given him access to the decision makers at every major race track in the world. His power over these people rendered facile the FIM's postulation that any track hosting a World Series event would be banned from holding FIM events and as laughable as their belief that they could renege on a deal with Bernie and get away with it!

IRTA have fared no better than the FIM in this sorry confrontation. Perhaps they thought that they could use Ecclestone to overcome the FIM, but if so they were disappointed as he assumed overall control of the bike Grands Prix. The situation for 1992, and for the next 10 years at least, it seems, is that the FIM will run the Grands Prix under Bernie Ecclestone's control. Ecclestone will negotiate with the circuit owners, who will pay him for the privilege of hosting a Grand Prix. Bernie will distribute the starting and prizemoney fund and will have control over all television and advertising rights. He will also promote each event through one of his companies. The FIM will govern the technical and sporting regulations, subject to Ecclestone's approval, and they will receive a small percentage of the overall receipts from each race to cover their expenses, but they will have no say in the distribution of prize, travelling or start monies. IRTA can continue to represent the teams and riders, but will have to negotiate with Ecclestone for any payments such as travelling money, and they will have little say in the running, promotion or technical regulations. ROPA, the promoters' association, appeared to have no role at all in the new scheme, and their spokesman, Maurizio Flammini, the Italian promoter of the World Superbike Championship, was brought into dispute with Ecclestone.

Meanwhile, a new organization has been formed, the International Sidecar Racing Association (ISRA), to negotiate with Bernie Ecclestone as representatives of the sidecar competitors.

This move came about because the sidecar riders felt very aggrieved that they had paid £30,000 in 1991 to IRTA for their representation, only for IRTA to be prepared to scrap the sidecar involvement in Grand Prix racing!

The plan for 1992 was that there would be eight or nine sidecar Grands Prix. These were to be held on the Saturday afternoon and televised, whereas the solo classes would race on Sundays. ISRA would have to guarantee the participation of 20 outfits at every round of the World Championship and conform to certain standards of competitiveness and appearance. In return, Bernie Ecclestone would pay an agreed amount to each crew at each race, plus prizemoney for the first 10 finishers.

Although Steve and several of his rivals make their living exclusively from their participation in the sidecar Grands Prix, none of them claimed to have been consulted during the negotiations concerning the future of GP racing. Having no factory affiliations and few large companies as sponsors, the sidecars entrants have had very little say with any of the ruling powers in GP racing. Instead, they complain to have been used by both sides in the power struggle when it suited them: ignored, abused and then ditched to fend for themselves. After being an integral part of GP racing for so many years, and having given so much excitement to countless thousands of fans, these so-often unsung heroes of motorcycle racing surely deserved better treatment.

Due to the dispute between the FIM and IRTA and the late intervention of Ecclestone, the Grand Prix calendar had still not been finalized in the first week of February, when the first race was thought to be only six weeks away. For the major 500cc teams this situation inevitably presented logistical problems, but for the privateers, and especially the sidecar racers, the difficulties were to be that much greater as they had to cope with the additional problem of trying to convince sponsors that the Grands Prix would actually happen at all!

The ongoing dispute between the warring factions of Grand Prix racing had a significant effect on Steve Webster's close-season preparations, and made a significant contribution to his winter of discontent. Steve knew that to remain competitive he would have to update his equipment, Rolf Biland's late-season pace having convinced him that the newer ADM design of engine was a necessity and that he also needed a new LCR chassis. It was after he had placed his orders for the new equipment that Webster was shocked to learn that his long-term sponsors, Levior, had decided not to renew his sponsorship for 1992. To add further to his worries, he was unable to contact Roland Munch and could not be certain that the German industrialist would continue his support into the new season. Furthermore, Steve's endeavours to find new sponsors were handicapped by the uncertainty surrounding the sidecars' continued participation at the highest level of the sport. Many potential sponsors were put off by the seemingly petty wrangling of the supposed rulers of bike racing. Large companies did not want to be associated with a sport which was in such turmoil because of the difficulty in justifying the expense to their shareholders.

It was the attempt to impress a potential sponsor that had indirectly led to the tragedy that claimed the life of Graham Rose. With Gavin in New Zealand to collect their World Championship medals, Steve had asked Graham to stand in at Brands Hatch, where the potential sponsor was to see the sidecar in action. However, because of Graham's death in practice the potential sponsor never did get to see the sidecar race and was never heard from again.

Graham's death had a far greater effect on Steve than he would be prepared to admit. Although he was in no way responsible, he blamed himself, and the reportage of the incident in the national press did nothing to ease his conscience. The combination of Graham's death, the uncertainty surrounding the World Championships and the difficulties with sponsorship all contributed to Steve's illness during the winter of 1991/92. He was admitted to hospital for tests, suffering from severe stomach pains. He had lost his appetite and was generally morose and depressed. For the first time in a decade he appeared to have lost his interest in sidecar racing. He deeply questioned his motivation and thought seriously about quitting, but his family and friends rallied round with support and encouragement, and slowly Steve emerged from his depression and started to make plans for the coming season. It was what Graham would have wanted.

Great Britain has had all too few representatives in the top echelon of motorcycle sport during the last decade. Of those who have been fortunate enough to reach the pinnacle of the sport and have done their best to represent themselves and their country, only Steve Webster has achieved any consistent level of success. Yet even after four World Championships to his credit, he remains the likeable, approachable, unassuming person that he has always been. His many fans have long felt that he has deserved far more recognition for his achievements, and much wider acknowledgement of his successes, than has come his way.

They must have been as gratified as he was, therefore, when in May 1992 they heard that he had been awarded the Segrave Trophy, one of Britain's most prestigious awards which commemorates Sir Henry Segrave, the famous racing driver and record-breaker, and honours annually the outstanding performance on land, water or in the air in the context of courage, skill, enterprise and achievement.

When the presentation was made at the Royal Automobile Club in London, it was pointed out that the magnificent trophy already carried the names of three distinguished motorcycle champions, Geoff Duke, who took the award in 1951, Barry Sheene, the winner in 1977 and again in 1984, and Mike Hailwood, who received it in 1979. But this was the first occasion when it had been won with the aid of three wheels – and, it was added, not a little help on the side – contributions which were rewarded by the presentation of special Segrave Medals to Gavin Simmons, Mick Webster and Mary Smith.

For Steve and his team it was a welcome relief from the growing tension which was continuing to build on the uncertainties of the 1992 season. Despite these, they had pressed ahead with plans to retain the title which Steve and Gavin had fought so hard for in 1991.

Their loyal sponsors Silkolene, Avon and AP Lockheed were prepared to continue their support, even though Steve could not confirm the extent of his racing activities as winter became spring and the solo classes embarked on their Grand Prix campaigns. After months of uncertainty, rumours, counter-rumours and endless promises, a calendar for the sidecar class was finally issued in early April. Two days later, however, this calendar was amended: there would be eight sidecar Grands Prix, but nobody could confirm that they would be run on the Sunday with the solo classes. During this chaotic period, when some sources suggested that the sidecars would race on Saturday evenings and others claimed that the sidecars would not race at all at the Grands Prix, but at the World Superbike or European Championship meetings, many sponsors had been reluctant to commit their money to a class that looked to be on the verge of extinction.

To keep faith with his sponsors and fans Steve decided to contest as many British Championship rounds as his truncated GP schedule would allow. Gavin and he took part in the open sidecar race at Donington Park, which was Steve's first British round for four years. The MRPC race supported the second round of the World Superbike Championship and provided the thousands of racegoers at the Leicestershire circuit with one of the most thrilling races they had ever seen. Steve and Gavin had been two seconds faster than their nearest competitors in practice, but in the race they put on a show for the crowd.

They diced with Steve Abbott and Shaun Smith for the entire 10 laps, the lead changing hands up to three times each lap, before Steve and Gavin forged ahead at the final corner to win by a single bike length, after 25 miles of breathtaking racing. The crowd certainly got their money's worth, although Gavin thought that Steve had left it far too late in his efforts to put on a good show for the fans! 'This was my first ever race win in England,' Gavin recounted later; 'I really thought that we weren't going to do it on that last lap – talk about brinkmanship!'

The first Grand Prix of the season was at the Jerez circuit in southern Spain on May 10, but to complete his pre-season preparations Steve first entered the two cash shoot-out races at Donington Park on May 3 and Brands Hatch on May 4. At each of these races there was £1,500 of prize money for the winner, a cool £3,000 if Steve could win both races, which would pay for the trip to Spain!

Steve and Gavin duly obliged, beating Darren Dixon on the Padgetts LCR Yamaha in each event. But the new-found speed of the Padgetts machine was a surprise and was not a flash in the pan, as Steve was to find out in Spain.

Immediately after the race at Brands Hatch the British sidecar contingent set off for Spain and the opening round of their World Championship. The solo riders had already contested three rounds of their series. At this point the sidecar riders had no passes to gain entry to the Jerez circuit, they had no detailed schedule for practice and had received no confirmation regarding how much prize and travelling money was to be paid. They arrived at Jerez to find that they had been put in a separate paddock from the solo competitors, with no access to the pits garages. They had been allocated just two practice sessions instead of the normal four, and still there was no news of the prizemoney.

Repeated attempts to clarify the situation received blank stares from the orgainzers. IRTA just ignored them, presumably in the hope that they would go away, and there was no-one available from TWP, Bernie Ecclestone's company, who could help them. The FIM promised to sort out the prizemoney situation, but said that it would take time because no-one was sure who was responsible for paying the sidecar racers!

At least they got to race, and what a race! Darren Dixon stormed to his first GP pole position when Steve had engine problems in the second practice session, after being two seconds clear in the first. At the start of the race Dixon converted his pole position into the lead of the race for the first five laps. Steve made a poor start, but slotted into fourth place at the first corner behind Dixon, Klaffenbock and Biland. Then Webster and Simmons fought past the outfits in front of them to take the lead on lap five and proceeded to pull away as the other front runners ran into tyre wear problems.

At the end of the 23-lap Grand Prix Webster and Simmons won by a margin of 17 seconds from Klaffenbock and Parzer. Biland failed to score but Barry Brindley claimed his first podium position in a GP after eight years of trying. There was little joy on the podium, however, as the various ruling bodies of the sport continued to give the class inadequate recognition – there was still no money available to them! Twenty sidecar crews had made the long journey to the south of Spain to take part in the GP, but none of them received a single peseta there for their efforts. Indeed, some of the poorer crews were left to wonder if they could afford the fuel for the long trip home!

The proposed GP schedule suggested that the sidecars would visit Hockenheim in Germany for their second round. However, after Spain a large number of the sidecar crews were saying they would not be able to afford to contest any more Grands Prix if the organizers failed to pay them prize and travelling money. Unlike the already well-financed solo classes, who had had a large increase in their prize fund, the sidecar competitors had to rely in the main on prize and appearance money to enable them to compete. The attitude of the governing bodies in Spain made it perfectly clear to them that there was no future for the amateur enthusiasts who make up the sidecar class. The three-wheelers might be able to survive the rest of the year, but in reality the writing seemed to be on the wall. It looked like the beginning of the end.

However, the sidecar crews duly turned up in Germany, where they found that the spectators had voted with their feet; the vast stands at the Hockenheimring looked almost deserted as protesters outside the circuit showed their displeasure at the huge increase in admission prices which had been forced on the circuits by the new regime and had priced the Grands Prix beyond so many motorcycle enthusiasts' reach. However, those who had found the money to attend were treated to a thrilling sidecar race on the ultra-fast slipstreaming circuit with Steve and Gavin grabbing a last-lap victory with an audacious overtaking manoeuvre at the tight left-hand corner in the stadium just as Klaffenbock was beginning to think that he had won. Darren Dixon and Andy Hetherington claimed third place in an equally close-fought battle with Japanese veteran Yoshi Kumagaya. Swiss ace Rolf Biland opened his 1992 account with eighth place after starting from pole position. In the Championship Webster and Simmons' perfect score of 40 points put them 10 points clear of Klaffenbock and Parzer; Kumagaya was third on 20 points whilst Biland's three points left him down in 10th place.

The eighth round of the solo championships and the third round for the sidecars took place at the Circuit van Drenthe at Assen in Holland. The Dutch TT races are historically the culmination of the Assen Speed Week, with European and National Championships being contested during the week prior to the Grand Prix. Despite the organizers' attempts to keep the admission prices down the crowd were vociferous in their condemnation of Bernie Ecclestone's new spectacle, many of them sporting T-shirts carrying suitably pointed messages to him.

During the meeting in Holland the FIM announced that the sidecar competitors would be paid travelling expenses for the 1992 Grands Prix but that the prizemoney situation had yet to be resolved. The FIM offered the sidecar class $50,000 US to divide between them at each round of the Championship, which was equivalent to about £1,000 per crew per meeting. For the first time in a decade Steve Webster's motivation appeared to have evaporated. The focus of his attention was no longer the World Championship; he was concerned only with financial survival. For over five years he had made a reasonable living from his racing; a Grand Prix win would net him around £6,000 in prize and travel money, which was enough for him to live on and to ensure the competitiveness of his machine. During 1992 Steve was losing money at every round he contested; even with his sponsorship from Avon Tyres, Silkolene Oils and his other smaller sponsors, he was having to pay to go racing just like in the old days of club racing!

The Dutch TT at Assen marked the turning point of the Championship with Rolf Biland finding the reliability to match his speed, and the veteran Swiss sidecar star showed all his class as he left the field trailing. Steve and Gavin were clear in second place, but could not put any pressure on Biland, who notched up his 61st Grand Prix victory.

The day after the Dutch TT the Yorkshire duo won a national race at Mallory Park, after travelling through the night from Holland. As pleasing as it was to win at Mallory, Steve knew that he had to find something to beat Biland at Grand Prix level, particularly as the Swiss former Champion's Yokohama tyres now appeared to have the edge over Steve's Avons.

The fourth round of the Championship in Hungary confirmed Steve's fears. Rolf's Yokohama tyres behaved perfectly through-out a race in which he led from lights to flag. Webster had to battle hard with Klaffenbock, also on Yokohamas, which made Steve's tyres deteriorate, and the reigning Champions only secured second position when the Austrian suffered gear selection problems. Steve explained that the new Yokohamas appeared not to lose grip as the race progressed, whereas he was having to push his tyres so hard that he was blistering them, with the result that his outfit was sliding more and more, which further overheated the tyres. Avon's technicians pondered the problem and vowed to produce some new compounds to match the threat from the Japanese tyre company.

Round five of the World Championship was held at the magnificent new Magny Cours circuit near Nevers, in Central France. Rolf Biland was once again in excellent form, converting his pole position into a hat-trick of race wins. His main opposition came from a very on-form Darren Dixon, who held second place for most of the race and recorded the fastest lap in his chase of Biland, but sadly, Darren's fine run came to nought when his machine let him down again. Webster's weekend was plagued with tyre troubles. He spun four times in practice and only managed a gripless fourth place in the race. Egbert Streuer was second, his first podium finish of the season, and Klaus Klaffenbock finished third to close the points deficit to Webster. Klaffenbock and Webster were separated now by only 14 points.

With the British Grand Prix as the next round, the Championship was finely poised, but ominous rumours began to circulate that the Donington race could be last for the sidecars – not just the last round of the 1992 World Championship, but the last ever sidecar World Championship race. The traumatic year had stumbled from one crisis to another as far as the sidecars were concerned. They were now receiving a small amount of money from the FIM, but they did not know if they would receive any prizemoney for this season. Indeed, they usually only knew that they were going to compete at 1992 Grands Prix a few days before each round occurred. As the teams assembled at Donington the rumours intensified; neither Brazil nor South Africa would stage sidecar races and there would be no Championship in 1993 although alternative races might be held in Holland, Italy and Spain, or somewhere … perhaps! No-one seemed to know what was happening. Then the counter rumours started: one was that the sidecars would race in Brazil because Hollywood cigarettes, sponsors of Biland and Streuer, had their biggest market in Brazil. They wanted more rounds so that Rolf, who was now looking unbeatable, could win the World Championship, whereas if Donington was to be the last round Steve Webster only needed to finish seventh to make sure of retaining his crown.

All the confusion regarding the future of the sidecars was beginning to have a serious effect on Steve. His motivation had been suspect for some time, but the two early season wins seemed to have fired him up. Now that Rolf was going so well and the future looked so uncertain, Steve was once again feeling less than 100 per cent focused on winning, and the additional pressure from fans and media at his home GP did nothing to lighten his mood.

As promised, Avon tyres produced three new compounds for Steve to try in an effort to overcome the excessive wheelspin which had caused him so many problems in the previous three GPs. Steve had also built a new engine for the British round, trying out some modifications to the squish band and porting in an attempt to match Biland's horsepower. Such experimentation from the man dubbed 'Mr Standard' was a further indication of Steve's turmoil. For the first time in 1992 Webster had two engines at this disposal and even if his off-track demeanor was slightly low-key and detuned, his on-track performance left no-one in any doubt about his determination and ability. Steve used the first untimed practice session to run-in his new engine and to scrub-in the new tyres which had only been delivered late on the Thursday evening. Steve declared himself pleased with the new tyre compounds, feeling that some progress had been made, but he was less sure of the engine, indicating that some more development would be necessary before a decision could be made.

The timed session on Friday afternoon saw Webster initially fastest, but he pulled into the pits early on feeling that all was not well with the engine. When Biland eclipsed his time Steve went back out onto the circuit, but could not better the Team Hollywood Sidecars near-lap record time and had to settle for second place on the provisional grid, just three tenths of a second slower than his Swiss rival. After practice a meeting with Bernie Ecclestone, attending only his second GP of the year, promised to iron out some of the problems afflicting the sidecar fraternity, but Steve still had that perennial problem to sort out – Biland!

The final practice session on Saturday afternoon was a disaster for Team Webster. Steve lost control in the windy conditions after only four laps into the session when he clipped the kerb at the gentle left-hander under Strakey's Bridge. The outfit drifted sideways onto the grass where it started to spin. Gavin realized that an accident was inevitable and bailed out, but he, like the machine, made heavy contact with the tyre wall on the outside of the circuit. Thankfully, neither driver nor passenger were seriously injured, both being lucky to sustain only bruises and abrasions. The outfit, however, came off far worse: the fairing was destroyed and the front suspension was badly damaged in the impact, which occurred at about 120mph. Indeed the damage was so extensive that Gavin had to be despatched to York to pick up brother Kevin's outfit so that the fairing and other vital pieces could be used to restore Steve's machine to a raceworthy condition.

The whole team, with help from Avon and Silkolene, buckled down to the task of rebuilding the crashed LCR, finally completing the repairs at 4 o'clock in the morning. It is worthy of mention that despite all that the sidecar competitors had been through during the season, the old camaraderie still remained. First on the scene as Webster returned to the paddock was Barry Brindley, eager to see if there was any way in which he could help and if there were any spares he had which Webster could utilize. It was a weary Team Webster that awoke on the day of the race to use the morning warm-up session to check if the machine had been set up properly after the abuse of the day before. More drama occurred during this warm-up when the ADM engine lapsed onto three cylinders. Number one cylinder was very wet, signifying perhaps that the plug was not firing, or that the carburation was too rich on that cylinder, or that there was a major problem with the reed valve or crankcase. This was Steve's original engine, the new one having been discarded because it was not revving properly.

The race turned into a benefit for Rolf Biland after he had resisted a challenge from Darren Dixon at the Old Hairpin on lap one. Webster moved past Dixon and settled into a secure second place, but was unable to close on Biland, who was dominating the fourth Grand Prix in a row. With two-thirds of the race run it became clear that Webster had a problem. Dixon was closing rapidly and Steve seemed powerless to prevent Darren taking his second place. Inevitably, Dixon and Hetherington passed Webster and Simmons and the crowd were urging on the ailing outfit of the gritty Yorkshire pair as they came under threat from the Egloffs and from Bonhorst and Hiller. Aided by some errant backmarkers, Steve and Gavin just held off the challenge from the German and Swiss pairings and emerged from Donington with third place and a nine-point lead in the Championship over Biland with now perhaps only one round to go. The engine had partially seized on one cylinder when a piston ring had become caught in one of the ports. The loss of those three points, it seemed, could well prove crucial!

In the days that followed the Donington race the situation regarding the Championship became more and more confused. Eventually it was decided that the sidecars could not journey to Brazil because the costs of shipping 24 outfits to South America were just too much. A round at the Assen Superbike meeting on September 13 was arranged to replace Brazil, and there was much talk about running a race in Spain to replace South Africa, where the organizers had stated quite clearly that they could not afford to cater for the chairs.

The meeting with Bernie Ecclestone, the FIM and IRTA produced some small comfort for the Cinderella class: the current year's prizemoney would be paid for all the rounds to an agreed scale, the class would continue at Grand Prix level for two more years and there would be eight races per year. In the run-up to the British Grand Prix Steve Webster had been contemplating his future, wondering if the sidecar class would continue and that if it was to die could he gain an additional wheel and get into car racing? However, the most recent announcement seemed to assure Steve's participation at the highest level of three-wheel racing for two more years at least, and give race fans worldwide the opportunity of seeing Britain's finest continue his battle with Rolf Biland, the greatest sidecar racer the world has ever seen. In the meantime it was on to Assen for what was to be the finale to the 1992 season's epic confrontation.

During the period between the British Grand Prix at Donington and the sidecar race at Assen the solo classes took part in their last two rounds of the 1992 season, at Interlagos in Brazil and Kyalami in South Africa. Luca Cadalora retained his 250cc title and the Italian youngster Alexandro Gramigni claimed the 125cc class for the small Italian manufacturers Aprilia. Against all the odds Wayne Rainey retained the Blue Riband crown after Mick Doohan had led the Championship all year. Mick's accident at Assen earlier in the season had forced him to miss several races, and although he contested the last two rounds he was not fit enough to carry the fight against Rainey.

Meanwhile, the situation in the sidecar arena was still fluid as the Assen meeting approached. No-one really knew whether the Dutch superbike meeting would be the last or the penultimate round in what had been a very tough year for the three-wheel racing fraternity. However, just five days before the crews assembled in Holland it was announced that the Dutch race would indeed be the last World Championship round in 1992. For Steve Webster the situation was clear: to retain his World Championship he had to finish third or better if Biland won, which on recent form seemed to be an odds-on certainty!

In qualifying at Assen, Rolf again achieved pole position, but Webster's new-compound Avon tyres had brought him much closer to Biland's pace, and from second place on the grid Steve was confident that he could do enough to retain his crown. For the first time in 1992 Webster and Simmons made a fantastic start and led the early laps quite comfortably from a hard-charging Biland, while the rest of the field were being outpaced. The Championship was beginning to look secure in the hands of the Yorkshire pairing. Eventually, Biland managed to force his way through to the front, but he was then faced with a major dilemma. He knew he could win the race, but with Webster in second place the Championship would stay in England. Rolf tried to slow the pace down in the hope that Streuer and Dixon could close the gap and find a way to overtake Webster but Steve maintained his position and on several occasions drew alongside and even ahead of the Swiss outfit. Biland's anxiety was growing and the Championship seemed to be fading from his grasp. If he kept going at a speed sufficient to stay in front there was no way that the other crews could keep up and affect the outcome of the Championship. Yet if he slowed down, Webster had the speed to overtake and pull away.

With two-thirds of the 26-lap race completed Biland led Webster by a very small margin and as the rest of the field were by now completely out of it, Webster seemed to be on course for the fifth World title. But, on lap 19, with seven to go, Biland and Waltisperg were suddenly on their own as Webster was seen limping towards the pits! The gear linkage on the Silkolene Team Webster outfit had fallen apart; the Championship was Biland's if he could finish the race. Lap 25 and Biland was slowing – was he in trouble? No, he was merely slowing down to let his friend and team-mate, Egbert Streuer, take the race win, knowing that the 15 points for second place would still give him the Championship by six points from Webster.

So the Swiss ace celebrated his fifth World Championship while the members of the Webster equipe were left to contemplate the remains of the £4 spherical joint that had failed and allowed the gear linkage to fall apart. Stamped on the mangled joint were the words SWISS MADE!

Sunday, September 13, 1992 was a black day for British motorsport enthusiasts as the newly crowned Formula One World Champion, Nigel Mansell, announced his retirement having failed to agree a deal with his employers, Williams Grand Prix Engineering. Britain should have had two World Champions that day, but in the fickle world of mechanized sport a £4 ball joint can be as important as a multi-cylinder engine or a well set up chassis in the overall performance of the machine.

Despite having the Championship snatched away from him in such a cruel fashion, Steve Webster remained philosophical in his moment of bitter disappointment: 'To be fair, Rolf deserves to win the Championship; he has been much quicker than anyone else since the third race of the season. I guess that this makes us even for 1988 when I pinched the Championship from him when he had mechanical trouble in the last race of the year!'

Although disappointed with the final outcome and disgusted with the treatment that the sidecar contingent as a whole had received during 1992, Steve was determined to redress the balance in 1993: 'The lack of prizemoney really affected us this year, although we had superb support from Silkolene, Avon and our smaller sponsors. We needed the prizemoney to top up our budget to allow us to compete on equal terms with Rolf. He was able to do the job properly, whereas we had to make do. If we can get this close on such a small budget, just think what we could do with a proper set-up. I'll be going all-out to add to my existing sponsorship so that I can repay the faith that they have shown in me. Meanwhile, we're going to take a holiday and try to forget all the problems of this year. Then we want the title back in 1993!'

Assuming they get the right backing, Webster and Simmons will once again be challenging Biland and Waltisperg, but the outlook for most of the other British crews was bleak indeed after their cruel 1992 season. For some of them the traumas had proved too much to bear, the lack of prize and travelling money having thrown them into bankruptcy. At the time of the Dutch GP each crew had received just £6,000 towards their expenses in return for their season's efforts, and although they had been promised that prizemoney on the 1991 scale would be paid in full, they were still awaiting it in mid-September.

For some, it was already too late. Abbott and Smith had been forced to give up and were trying to sell their entire equipment in an attempt to cover the debts they had incurred; Darren Dixon had decided to switch back to two wheels because he felt he could make more money from finishing last in a 500cc solo Grand Prix than he could from winning a sidecar round!

As for Webster, if he had decided to continue his studies, he might well have pondered on the personal appropriateness of those immortal opening lines from Shakespeare's *Richard III*, because 1992 had most certainly been his 'Winter of Discontent'. One could only hope that this particular 'Son of York' could put it all behind him and likewise make it a 'Glorious Summer' in 1993. Five times a World Champion? Of one thing we could all be sure – he would be giving it his best shot!

Appendix

Steve Webster's competition record

1979 – First race: Auto 66 Club – Passenger: Kevin Webster – Fidderman/Suzuki 750

1981 – Winner Auto 66 Club Championship – Passenger: Kevin Webster – Windle/Yamaha 750

1982 – Winner Marlboro Clubmans Championship – Passenger: Tony Hewitt – Windle/Yamaha 750

1983 – First Grand Prix – Great Britain (Silverstone) – 5th – Passenger: Tony Hewitt – Windle/Yamaha 500

1985 – British Champions – Passenger: Tony Hewitt – LCR/Yamaha

1986 – First Grand Prix win – Belgium (Spa Francorchamps) – British Champions – Passenger: Tony Hewitt – LCR/Yamaha

1987 – World Champions – British Champions – Passenger: Tony Hewitt – LCR/Krauser

1988 – World Champions – British Champions – Passenger: Tony Hewitt/Gavin Simmons (Czechoslovakia) – LCR/Krauser

1989 – World Champions – Passenger: Tony Hewitt – LCR/Krauser

1990 – Third in World Championship – Passenger: Gavin Simmons – LCR/Krauser

1991 – World Champions – Passenger: Gavin Simmons – LCR/Krauser

1992 – Second in World Championship – Winner *Motor Cycle News* Supercup – Passenger: Gavin Simmons – LCR/ADM

Grand Prix results:

1983:

Great Britain (Silverstone)	5th
Sweden (Anderstorp)	14th
San Marino (Mugello)	DNF
World Championship position:	16th

1984:

Austria (Salzburgring)	DNF
West Germany (Hockenheim)	3rd
France (Le Mans)	DNF
Holland (Assen)	11th
Belgium (Spa-Francorchamps)	10th
Great Britain (Silverstone)	DNF
Sweden (Anderstorp)	DNF
World Championship position:	8th

1985:

West Germany (Hockenheim)	2nd
Austria (Salzburgring)	3rd
Holland (Assen)	DNF
Sweden (Anderstorp)	3rd
World Championship position:	4th

1986:

West Germany (Nurburgring)	DNF
Austria (Salzburgring)	2nd
Holland (Assen)	2nd
Belgium (Spa-Francorchamps)	1st
France (Le Mans)	3rd

Great Britain (Silverstone)	2nd
Sweden (Anderstorp)	15th
West Germany (Hockenheim)	3rd
World Championship position:	3rd

1987:

Spain (Jerez)	1st
West Germany (Hockenheim)	1st
Austria (Salzburgring)	4th
Holland (Assen)	2nd
France (Le Mans)	3rd
Great Britain (Donington)	1st
Sweden (Anderstorp)	2nd
Czechoslovakia (Brno)	3rd
World Championship position:	1st

1988:

Spain (Jerez)	3rd
West Germany (Hockenheim)	2nd
Austria (Salzburgring)	3rd
Holland (Assen)	3rd
Belgium (Spa-Francorchamps)	2nd
France (Paul Ricard)	2nd
Great Britain (Donington)	1st
Sweden (Anderstorp)	1st
Czechoslovakia (Brno)	1st
World Championship position:	1st

1989:

USA (Laguna Seca)	1st
West Germany (Hockenheim)	1st
Austria (Salzburgring)	15th
Holland (Assen)	1st
Belgium (Spa-Francorchamps)	2nd
France (Paul Ricard)	2nd
Great Britain (Donington)	1st
Sweden (Anderstorp)	3rd
Czechoslovakia (Brno)	3rd
World Championship position:	1st

1990:

USA (Laguna Seca)	2nd
Spain (Jerez)	1st
Italy (Misano)	2nd
West Germany (Nurburgring)	1st
Austria (Salzburgring)	2nd
Yugoslavia (Rijeka)	3rd
Holland (Assen)	DNF
Belgium (Spa-Francorchamps)	6th
France (Le Mans)	1st
Great Britain (Donington)	DNF
Sweden (Anderstorp)	4th
Czechoslovakia (Brno)	2nd
World Championship position:	3rd

1991:

USA (Laguna Seca)	1st
Spain (Jerez)	1st
Italy (Misano)	1st
Germany (Hockenheim)	DNF
Austria (Salzburgring)	1st
Spain (Jarama)	1st
Holland (Assen)	DNF
France (Paul Ricard)	2nd
Great Britain (Donington)	2nd
San Marino (Mugello)	2nd
Czechoslovakia (Brno)	3rd
France (Le Mans)	3rd
World Championship position:	1st

1992:

Spain (Jerez)	1st
Germany (Hockenheim)	1st
Holland (Assen)	2nd
Hungary (Hungaroring)	2nd
France (Magny Cours)	4th
Great Britain (Donington)	3rd
Holland (Assen)	DNF
World Championship position:	2nd

The reward ...

1O DOWNING STREET
LONDON SW1A 2AA

From the Principal Private Secretary

4 May 1990

Sir,

    The Prime Minister has asked me to inform you, in
strict confidence, that she has it in mind, on the
occasion of the forthcoming list of Birthday Honours, to
submit your name to The Queen with a recommendation that
Her Majesty may be graciously pleased to approve that you
be appointed a Member of the Order of the British Empire.

    Before doing so, the Prime Minister would be glad to
be assured that this would be agreeable to you. I should
be grateful if you would let me know by completing the
enclosed form and sending it to me by return of post.

    If you agree that your name should go forward and
The Queen accepts the Prime Minister's recommendation,
the announcement will be made in the Birthday Honours
List. You will receive no further communication before
the List is published.

                I am, Sir,
                Your obedient Servant,

                ANDREW TURNBULL

S Webster Esq
Flanwith Service Station
Flanwith
Alne
York

INVESTITURE H

22nd June 1990

Sir,

I am commanded to inform you that an Investiture will be held at Buckingham Palace on Wednesday, 25th July, 1990 at which your attendance is requested.

I am desired to say that you should arrive at the Palace between the hours of 10 o'clock and 10.30 a.m. and this letter should be shown on entering the gates of the Palace, and at the Grand Hall Entrance of the Palace, as no other card of admission is issued to recipients. Cars may be parked in the inner Quadrangle of the Palace under police direction. A Car Parking Label is enclosed herewith.

You are permitted to bring with you TWO guests (relations or friends) to watch the Ceremony. This number may be increased to THREE only if your guests are your spouse and two children (of your own). In NO circumstances can this number be increased. Tickets for them may be obtained by making application on the form enclosed herewith which should be returned to me as soon as possible.

DRESS

(a) Serving Officers and Other Ranks of the Royal Navy, Royal Marines, Army, Royal Air Force and Members of the Police Force and Fire Brigades should wear the dress laid down in the regulations of their respective Service. Decorations and Medals should not be worn; nor should swords be worn.

(b) Retired Officers who are not in possession of the dress described in *(a)* should wear Morning Dress or Dark Lounge Suit. Orders, Decorations and Medals should not be worn.

(c) Civilians may, *if they so desire,* wear the uniform of the Civil Organization or Service to which they belong; otherwise they should wear Morning Dress or Dark Lounge Suit. Orders, Decorations and Medals should not be worn.

I am, Sir,

Your obedient servant,

Malcolm Ross
Lieutenant Colonel

Secretary

Stephen Webster Esq., MBE

The congratulations ...

DEPARTMENT OF THE ENVIRONMENT
2 MARSHAM STREET LONDON SW1P 3EB
01- 276 3000

My ref

Your ref

16 JUN 1988

Mr S Webster
3 Highland Court
Easingwold
York
YO6 3QL

Dear Steve,

It gives me great pleasure to write and congratulate you on the
award of MBE to you in the Birthday Honours.

I know that you have devoted much time and effort to the services
of sport and I am delighted that this has now been recognised in
this way.

Yours sincerely,

Colin.

COLIN MOYNIHAN